SOULMATE
DOG

Michelle B. Slater, Ph.D.

Soulmate Dog

Published in the United States by Wandering Cloud Press
www.wanderingcloudpress.com

Cover Portrait by Caleb Smith

Ebook, Hardcover, and Paperback cover design
by The Book Cover Whisperer
www.openbookdesign.biz

Audiobook by Alison Larkin Presents
alisonlarkinpresents.com

Interior Book Design by Inanna Arthen
inannaarthen.com

Library of Congress Control Number: 2024902273

ISBN 978-1-963452-00-6 (paperback)
ISBN 978-1-963452-01-3 (hardcover)
ISBN 978-1-963452-02-0 (ebook)

PRAISE FOR SOULMATE DOG

Michelle B. Slater gives us the moving story of a deep love connection with her German Shepherd that highlights the important role of holistic veterinary medicine and animal communication in her engaging book, *Soulmate Dog*."

–Penelope Smith, Animal Communicator

"You will love Brady and his soulmate, Michelle. Their journey together – one filled with joy and pain and, ultimately, transformative triumph – will inspire you to be a more grateful, mindful, courageous and loving human."

–Sy Montgomery, author of *How to Be A Good Creature*

"Considering how most animals, wild and domesticated, are treated today, the doors of perception are closed. Thanks to Dr. Slater for offering this engaging book to open these doors. I wish for everyone to experience the love of a being other than human and to give that love and respect back to all creatures great and small."

–Michael W. Fox, Author and Veterinarian

Dedication

For Snow

TABLE OF CONTENTS

Preface

Soulmate Dog charts the nature of love and the inevitability of loss that accompanies it. It delves into the depths of love as I experienced it. And who was I loving? I didn't fully understand what a dog was until I started learning the language of Dog. A certain dog, the "one" dog that challenged my entire philosophical education, and I relate our journey together here. And as we went, we learned pivotal lessons, including about how love makes us willing to go to extraordinary lengths in our care, as I did for a dog named Brady. But when you have read through the heft of the book that you now hold in your hand, it won't leave you alone to grieve what may have been your own losses—or even to empathize with mine that may have touched you. Rather, it gently takes you through the messiness of grief on a raw healing journey.

This book is for anyone who has ever loved an animal or theorized about an animal's faculties and concluded that a dog is not just a dog. It is for anyone who has experienced unparalleled love between a dog and a human. It's a celebration of soulmate dogs.

Chapter One
The Vicissitudes of Joy and Grief

I once asked my parents for a sibling for Christmas. I was then eight. "It could be a brother or a puppy," I stipulated. I saw little difference, and either would have pleased me enormously. But as it happened, that Christmas, I pulled no baby of any species from my stocking. A disappointment. But animals continued to enter our household another way, thanks to our family reading nights where we'd pile into my parents' bed and my naturalist mother would read. One book she chose then has stayed with me all my life: *In the Shadow of a Rainbow*, written by Robert Franklin Leslie. If I was a child yearning for an interspecies sibling relationship with a dog—making no distinction between a human or a nonhuman animal—Leslie's book confirmed that way of seeing the world.

On these evenings, my father and I would sit on either side of my mother, I curled against her, as she read the story of a courageous man who befriended a wolf in the wilds of British Columbia. Her voice, dulcet and flexible from years of singing and the acting she'd done as a girl, lent itself to reading out loud. This narrative mesmerized us, and we listened to her for hours each night as we traveled from New England to the wilds of Canada.

In the book, Leslie recounts the story of a young man in British Columbia, Gregory Tah-Kloma, a young Inuit man who developed an intimate relationship with a notorious female wolf pack leader, Náhani—or, one who shines—a great silver wolf that was fallaciously infamous for killing men, and destroying their trap lines. Greg forged his way for hundreds of miles through the remote wilderness to save this majestic pack of wolves before trappers and bounty hunters destroyed them. Something clicked between Greg and Náhani, and after hours of silent communication, this 140-pound wolf—that Greg had witnessed fighting with grizzly bears—jumped and placed her paws on his shoulders, and licked his nose. I giggled in delight as Mom read this. She patted my head as she continued. The relationship between the man and the wolf deepened over the course of several seasons, as Greg went to extreme measures to seek out Náhani and her elusive pack.

In a notable anecdote that demonstrates the wolf's commitment to Greg, Náhani killed a member of her wolf pack that was about to kill him. The attacking wolf was in a deranged state after having suffered an injury inflicted by a steel trap; she lunged at Greg when he tried to help her. I squirmed at this and nestled my head on my mom's lap, while she continued. Thinking back on her reading as an adult, I realize that Náhani and Greg's ability to commune showed Greg that he was partly instinctual like an animal, and that Náhani's ability to reason was incontrovertible. He became more animalesque and she became more humanesque the more they interacted with one another.

Náhani showed dog-like pleasure when she saw Greg, by wagging her tail at his presence. "That's extraordinary," Dad whispered. "Please keep reading, Mom," I said, tugging on her sleeve. In spite of her supreme alpha status, which Greg accepted unquestionably, Náhani rolled on her back and allowed him to remove thistles and thorns from her vulnerable underbelly and between her paws, and she let him groom her.

The nature of their friendship is epitomized by one midnight walk, instigated by Náhani pulling Greg's jeans with her teeth, her established signal for him to follow her. Twenty-eight wolves joined them, and Greg was flanked by four wolf guards for several miles as the pack inspected the circumference of the lake, illuminated by the full moon. Greg's journal entry from that night exemplifies the extraordinary nature of the wolf: "It was Náhani's superb control of the pack. She had the whole thing planned last night when she came into camp. Every wolf knew what was going to happen. Náhani now has shown me how a wolf thinks. In Youngpine's native Penutian legend [...] when anything strengthens a bond of friendship, Chimmesyans say the friends have walked in the shadow of a rainbow."[1] I was in awe of this wild wolf, her young Inuit friend, and their campfire "conversations" where they each allowed themselves to be vulnerable enough to sleep next to one another, while Náhani's pack slept close by. When Mom tucked me in that night, I said, "*I* yearn to walk in the shadow of a rainbow with a wolf like her."

The rapport between Náhani and Greg Tah-Kloma formed the philosophical underpinnings of what I understood as the relationship between humans and nonhuman animals. I thought of wolves and dogs as great beings from whom I had much to learn, and I felt like a humble child in deference to them. I knew that my parents did, too, based on our discussions. Thanks to the story of Náhani and Tah-Kloma, I knew then that I would always respect the mysterious intelligence and transcendent beauty of wolves. I hoped that I would meet someone like Náhani one day, or at least a lupine-like dog.

One afternoon, a dog wandered into our yard without a collar, shy yet affable. I tumbled out the door onto the lawn to greet it, hugging its black neck and petting its tan head. "It may not return your affection," my mother called after me, but it did. The dog accepted my hugs and extended its dirt-encrusted paw to me. "May we keep him, Mom?" I asked. "We may not, but we'll make sure he finds his way home," she promised. The dog spent a few nights with us while my mother attempted to locate his family. Since he was such a good sport about accepting my ever-present attention, I called him Trooper. *Perhaps if I name him, he'll get to stay,* I thought.

Alas, Trooper was not to be my sibling, for my mother found a home for him. I cried when his new family came to take him away. "I wonder if Trooper's children hug him like I did?" I would ask. "I'm sure he's a happy boy," Mom reassured me.

Soon after, one weekday evening, my parents announced that we were going on a field trip to an undisclosed location. This was an anomaly, and Mom was singing and smiling as she put a few odd things in the car, like a towel and a blanket. My father had a Christmas morning look on his face, and he was in the car before anyone else, eager to depart.

The field trip didn't seem enchanting at all. We drove an hour before pulling up to an unassuming house in a rural area. Dad and I stayed in the car while Mom disappeared through the front door. Dad's ebullient nature could never contain a secret—he often gave away Christmas presents he just couldn't wait until late December to give—but he stayed very quiet in the car. If I could have seen his face from the back seat in the dark, I imagine he would have been pursing his lips together. After a while he called out in a joyful tone, "Close your eyes, Michelley." I could tell through my closed eyelids that he had turned the lights on in the car, and then I heard Mom opening the car to the back seat. I kept my eyes closed until it felt like there was a large baby chick on my lap.

"Ahhhh!" I squealed. The breath stopped at my lungs and my face quivered with wonder. "She's all yours, forever!" Dad said with jubilation, reaching his hand back to pet my new soft friend who had already molded to my lap. "She's a German shepherd puppy, just like you dreamed of," Mom said proudly. I couldn't speak. Enraptured. I was enraptured. I beamed at them.

I lowered my head and murmured as I stroked the puppy's downy fur. She peered into my eyes, and licked my nose and cheeks with her tiny tongue as an introduction. "Joy, joy, joy," I finally said, before remembering to thank them, which I did every day for months.

Mom registered her in the American Kennel Club as Joyful Naháni, but we called her Joy for short. I liked to imagine that she was a descendent of the fiercely wise yet tender Naháni. She wasn't really all mine, either, because my parents loved her as much as I did. In that way she was like a true sibling. We shared her, and she grew to be our matriarch alongside my mom.

Looking back, I can still see the light that she brought to all of us. Mom took Joy with us for day hikes on the Appalachian Trail. Dad praised her and slipped her morsels of New York strip steaks. "Michael! You're training her to beg!" Mom half-protested, half-smiled. "Ohh, she will never have to beg," Dad mollified her. Mom brushed her coat while she sang to her, making up lyrics about a special dog. I played my saxophone for her, practicing the études and pieces my teacher Kenneth Radnofsky taught me every week at New England Conservatory. Joy would listen to me practice for hours. She loved us with a gentle kindness that still exudes nobility in my memory.

My mother was always singing and playing the piano it seemed. There was one hymn that was a leitmotif in our home, and it comes from Psalms: "Weeping may endure for a night, but joy cometh in the morning." Looking back, I wonder if it was a preparatory gift of consolation from her, for when I was forced to grieve her untimely death as a teenager, [of 14] — one so innocent I hadn't yet held a boy's hand, but who still held my mom's hand with unabashed affection as we crossed the street.

My mother, who taught me how to identify wildflowers, animal tracks, and stars, and to love all creatures, left us abruptly on the last day of November, shortly after the Berlin Wall fell. She never spoke of her fragile heart, and I wouldn't have understood the concept since she loved us all so fiercely that I only ever saw her strength. The interplay between strength and fragility was implicit in my family, but one that wasn't adumbrated with words.

I have never quite grown skin over the crater her absence created in my heart.

One day, sometime after my mother had died, I played a cassette I had made from radio songs that I liked. I listened to Tracy Chapman sing relaxed strains of "Fast Car," until Chapman's voice was replaced with the sound of a hand moving over a surface, followed by my mother singing a lilting song: "You're a dirty doggie! You're just a dirty doggie!" I must have left the tape playing when I left the house, and when my mother went to turn it off after a muddy walk with Joy, she accidentally hit record instead of stop. The sound of my mother's voice — playful, pure, the epitome of love — sent me into another round of tears behind the drawn curtains on my canopy bed.

Lost to me forever, I sobbed into Joy's back. She snuggled beside me, a place she no longer left. I curled my body around hers as I listened to Rachmaninov's second piano concerto on repeat — it was my musical consolation and I couldn't sleep without it playing throughout the night. The fur of Joy's back was soaked by my tears, but I had no way of telling her that our primary person was never coming back, and that it wasn't her fault.

One afternoon, I made hot chocolate. As I stared absentmindedly at two teal ceramic mugs of hot chocolate on the counter, I realized that I had made one for Mom, too. The weeping became whimpering. Joy licked the tears from my cheeks, but I couldn't stop producing them. I knew I was crying for both of us.

My weeping doubled when I went back to school where I was studying music at Interlochen Arts Academy, a boarding school for the arts in northern Michigan. I still didn't fully comprehend that my mother wasn't coming back, and I grieved not being able to take Joy with me. Guilt came in my suitcases instead. *I should have taken care of Joy for Mom,* I thought to myself every day. I asked for a single room so that no one would hear me cry at night, but my request was denied purposefully, so that I wouldn't be alone. I cried in the Northern Michigan woods, resting my soggy cheek on the crisp bark of sugar maple trees that reminded me of Mom and our winter walks with Joy.

When I played my saxophone and read books, an invisible valve opened up, letting some of the grief out. Palpable and constant, grief began to seem like an autonomous entity, and a powerful one, so I started thinking of it as Grief. When I read Dostoevsky's *Brother's Karamazov* in my junior year, I cleaved to his theme that became my new mantra: *you can't know joy unless you have known suffering, otherwise you wouldn't know it was joy.*

There needs to be a distinction. Odd as it sounds, that consoled me, for I had known joy. I knew joy as our tiny nuclear family exuded it, comprised of a dog and three humans. I knew joy in the tireless love my mother extended to all of us. Now I knew how much it had really meant. And I felt I would never get it back.

Those high school years passed with me flying off the plane to greet Dad and Joy for holiday vacations, until one day that he came to pick me up, she wasn't in the car.

"Daddy," I asked. "Where's Joy?"

He choked, something my eloquent dad just didn't do. "She went to be with your mother."

"What? You mean she *died*? Why didn't you tell me?" I said, a panicky feeling brewing in my chest.

"You had finals and your senior recital. I didn't want you to be alone finding out," he croaked. Tears seeped from his ocean blue eyes.

"Daddy, I can't bear it. I didn't get to say goodbye!" I wailed. "She must have thought I abandoned her, Dad. I *needed to be there.*" I began to cry.

"She knew that you loved her, just like your mother knew." And then, with confidence, he offered: "You'll see her again one day. You'll all be together one day."

But it didn't mitigate my pain. It didn't fill in my holes. Like a dog, I was a present-moment person, and my present was marked by screams of "absence, absence." I couldn't count on some spurious future in another dimension.

I learned that Dad had come home from work one day to find that Joy had died in the house. She had been alone. Joy hadn't shown any signs of being ill in the previous days, and I conjecture that without Mom being home with her every day, without me being there, and with Dad working long hours as an attorney, she died of a lonely, broken heart. *Joy and Mom went together and now they are both gone,* I lamented.

Those words, as honest as I could render them, seem too neatly arranged for Grief. Even now, just writing them, I had the urge to vomit, to run from my desk to the sea where I see dogs and their people on a winter walk on the Outer Cape, to cry out to the ocean: "I still can't digest and assimilate what happened." More than three decades have passed, and I still can't reason my way out of it as an adult. The childlike part that's still inside of me wasn't consoled in a way that mitigated Grief.

For weeks after my mother's death, I looked for an obituary every day in the paper, but Dad had been too stunned by the suddenness of her death to write one. The same went for a funeral. Closure was nowhere for me.

And Dad. My pillar—emotionally, not physically, since he had long suffered the effects of post-polio syndrome—had never been so toppled. Broken. Like an ancient ruin.

I couldn't let it all out when I was a child—no, that wouldn't have done—because I couldn't fall apart for my dad.

My strategy at the time was to shine for him. Without support for my grief, but without even knowing I had no support, or that I required support, I made sure that my grades stayed up and my musical performances were successful. That meant I could only have mini-episodes of falling apart, like running down snowy trails, howling in my concert performance attire, only to return to my rehearsal or practice with renewed focus.

Eventually, my dad would come to excel at being a professional dad. But back then, he was still stumbling to navigate his own grief. He had lost his own mom when he was 23, and he'd loved my mother as if she were more angel than human. And so he, the main adult in my life, wasn't able to fully support me in those first years after her death, and so Grief continues to spill over now that I'm writing about it, 31 years later.

Now, as an adult, when I go back to guest teach at Interlochen, I offer my students (all high-level artists) meditations to help them better tolerate distress. I guide them to bring up their fearful, anxious, or sad feelings and breathe into them as they acknowledge them. They don't try to get away from the distress or shift it; they just experience it. What they find is that distress shifts once it has been acknowledged and experienced. Once it has been supported. I didn't know how to do any of that when I was their age.

At Interlochen, Bill Sears, my saxophone teacher, thought that he made me cry during our weekly private lessons, but I reassured him years later at an alumni reception that I experienced mini-spills, like oil spills only made out of tears, and sometimes I couldn't control them. I could control the collateral damage to those around me though, because I never rebelled like many teenagers do. I couldn't cause more Grief for Dad. When I thought I might drown from the spills, I walked over to see my academic mentor, Monsieur M, otherwise known as James Murphy, outside of French class. He let me express my sadness, but only in French, which I did while he nodded with his kind eyes.

Even now, I feel a spill coming on. I want to close my eyes, drop my pen, curl into myself like a dog sleeping on a rainy day, and not share the salty residue of childhood tears that still stain my face.

But the residue is forever with me, in the form of my journal entries and essays, written just days after my mother died. Perhaps I had a premonition that my memory could be subject to nostalgia's edits, so I tried my hand early at writing about Grief. I share this entry, unedited, from December 11, 1989, written 12 days after my mother's death:

I am enshrouded in a dream world. I am unable to see a path out of my dreams, or see any glimpse of reality. My fellow companions, and family stare in at me from all around, but I am unable to see out. They appear concerned about me, but make no attempts to rescue me. I gaze out at the hazy clouds surrounding me. The clouds always show pictures of my mother and me together. Sometimes we're just shopping, or decorating the Christmas tree. At other times, I see myself sick, with my mother watching, caring, and comforting me. Then, I will see her singing to me, with her beautiful soprano voice that sounds like honey, when she showers me with notes overflowing with love. These wonderful clouds never rob me of my mother, and I see myself with her every waking moment. My problem solver, dissolving all of my pain and sadness, she has never left my side, and my peaceful clouds never hint that she will. I love my dream world, and never want to see past my past memories that I am so fond of.

An unknown force suddenly grips me, rudely yanking me out of my refuge. A cold, icy wind creeps over my body, leaving no thoughts of comfort or peace. The constant gusts of wind feel like knives, tearing my world apart. I am all alone, paralyzed and blind. An evil voice shouts to me from all around, therefore concealing its origin. The voice tells me that I will never see, feel, or hear my mother again. Sadness spreads throughout my body, bones, and veins, replacing my warm blood with ice water. Together with loneliness, I am shredded, left defenseless, and I blindly grope for my mother. She is nowhere to be found. This breaks my heart into thousands of pieces, and they scatter, now lost forever, irretrievable. Reality is overcoming any stray wisp of my former world of dreams. One message is conveyed to my brain, over and over again, until it is pulsating throughout my soul and body, leaving me too weak to tremble. I am crushed under the weights of affection, misery, and grief. Misery cancels out all affection. I feel like a living corpse. The pulsating message is still beating, an artificial heart, and one that will never cease to torment me. It shouts at me, with evil; passionate and merciless, it coldly yells at me. My mother is dead.

Just as I think I can't share this, little cairns appear before me, guiding me on this writing path.

As Grief revivified itself on the page, I took an afternoon break from writing and read Martin Amis's *Inside Story*, and fell upon advice that seemed meant for me: "My father Kingsley had a nice introductory formula on sensitive subjects. It was: 'Talk about it as much as you like or as little as you like.'"[2] This offering consoled me, and I thought I could offer a pithy chapter, without going into the messy details of my childhood grief.

Like when I called my dad from the dorm hall phone at Interlochen, telling him I missed Mom, and his cryptic reply was, "But she was never in that body; she is a divine creation that is eternal."

I said, "Then who was that woman who sang 'the muffins are ready' to me to the melody of a Beethoven piano sonata? Who handpicked the blueberries for the muffins, and took them out of the oven? Who stayed up all night decorating panda bear cakes for my birthday?" (The philosopher in me would have asked today, "Was she an automaton?")

His strategy was to intellectualize his grief through an esoteric belief system he since moved on from, thankfully. What I didn't know was that Dad didn't know how to grieve either, but he kept calling, kept praising my efforts in school, kept telling me he loved me every time we said goodbye, kept taking me to places, like the ocean, where I could be soothed.

On the night I learned that Joy had died, retroactively, I didn't have *her*, my best solace in the years since my mom had died. My old Rachmaninov recording helped me make it through the night. When I woke the following morning,

Dad had left for the office, but I needed to be with someone who loved me that day. I found my old bicycle, and on an impulse, without telling anyone, I biked over the river and through the woods for 50 miles until I pedaled up Brock Hill—named after my mother's maiden surname—and the antique white cape overlooking the Presidential range came into sight. I was 17 and I had just graduated from high school the week before.

This was the home of my mother's parents. My grandmother appeared outside, peering at me as if I were a mirage. "Michelle? Is that you? Did you come all the way here on your bicycle?" Her Scottish lilt put incredulity into each syllable. Grandpa appeared behind her, saying: "Well, it's my little French girl." I hugged Grandma first, and then, as she moved aside, I put my head on Grandpa's shoulder without saying a word. There was no word to be said. The gesture told him. "She was a good dog. We'll go for a walk in the woods after lunch," came his reply. This was our language of grief.

Another cairn appeared just yesterday, guiding me through the writing of Grief. My dear friend Raphael's father died in France. A father that had been his model, his giant, his beloved. I lit a candle for Monsieur Milan, and sent a photo of it to Raphael. He replied (in French): "I think about you again, and the courage it took you to overcome the loss of your mother so young. You are proof of resilience, a word that Boris Cyrulnik has written a lot about."

Raphael wasn't the first to tell me I was the embodiment of what Cyrulnik meant by resilience. I knew exactly what words he was referring to: "We have always been astonished by children who succeed in surviving terrible ordeals and making something of themselves against all odds."[3] He goes on to ask: "How do we become human despite the blows of fate?" In my case, as an adult, it was all about a dog, which I'm getting to, which I'm framing for you.

But my early lessons in resilience came from Mom, from Dad, Joy, Grandma and Grandpa, Monsieur M, from my childhood saxophone teacher Kenneth Radnofsky, and from a candle of light inside me that I kept lit with the help of my music, my books, nature, and my love for animals. But one never knows just how resilient one will have to be, or for how long.

I missed Joy through college, and through grad school, too. I just didn't talk about it very much. Neither did my father, and I couldn't broach our shared grief because his crater was so massive, he couldn't talk about it. And fresh grief widened my own crater when Grandpa died from an aneurysm well into his 90s. Even though his New England reserve didn't permit him to say he loved me, I knew that he did, and that comforted me even with his absence, when I had no dog to cry on.

One day a dog will come to me, I comforted myself. Sometimes I thought I didn't deserve to be graced with another dog, since I had failed to be there for Joy when she needed me most, but I still dreamed of it. *I will love that dog and stay by its side through hurricanes and starbursts of light. I won't betray her by going away to boarding school when she needs me the most. I won't betray her by not being there if she gets sick.*

Chapter Two
Brady: The "One" Dog

Decades passed. Now in my 30s, I was having dinner with my Russian-born beau who I had met at Dartmouth, Dmitri, and another couple, when the conversation turned to our shared love for German shepherds. "They were family members, our shepherds!" Roxanne asserted, thumping the table. Her childhood sweetheart Paul nodded his shaggy head, looking like he was recalling fond memories of them. The conversation continued with Dmitri sharing how he had grown up with both German shepherds and gargantuan Caucasian mountain shepherds in Moscow. He said, "I would love to have a big dog, but I would probably end up being the one to take care of it." A facetious quip, I surmised, but I drifted inside while my dinner companions continued talking about dogs.

Whenever I saw a German shepherd, or a big dog smiling up at its human, the guilt of not being by Joy's side during her final days iced my heart once again, even on the most sweltering days in Baltimore, where I earned my Ph.D. at Johns Hopkins. During that time, I had learned what the best philosophers had to say about nonhuman animals, and I had written my dissertation partially on Milan Kundera. Kundera's character Tereza was disconsolate when her dog Karenin's cancer spread, as he describes in *The Unbearable Lightness of Being*: "The love she bore her dog made her feel cut off, isolated. With a sad smile, she told herself that she needed to hide it more than she would an affair. People are indignant at the thought of someone loving a dog."[4] Kundera uses Tereza's love for Karenin to explain how philosophy had relegated the dog to being far beneath humans, and then he makes a point that others have made: "mankind's true moral test, its fundamental test, consists of its attitude towards those who are at its mercy: animals."[5] These ideas became pivotal in my philosophical formation. I read what all of the philosophers had to say about dogs. And at the time, I discussed them with Dad, who agreed with Kundera.

Through those years, Dad grew into being a professional dad, and his love sustained me as if he had doubled his roles as both Dad and Mom. There was nothing I couldn't talk to him about; no subject was verboten. He eloquently honored Grandpa at his funeral when I was studying at Dartmouth, showing me that he had learned to navigate Grief.

After dinner with our friends that night, I decided to heal the old emotional wound by adopting a German shepherd. In graduate school I had been too focused on my studies to be responsible for a dog, but I had just been awarded my doctorate six months ago, and it was time. I resolved to be there for my future hypothetical canine companion through thick and thin. D—as I had nicknamed Dmitri—agreed that a puppy would be good for us. We launched our search for the "one" dog.

One wintry night in January, the month of auspicious beginnings, D and I drove across three state lines to meet an eight-pound German shepherd puppy on the border of New Jersey and Pennsylvania. I was conflicted for I felt a moral obligation to adopt a rescue dog, but on the other hand I felt I had unfinished business with German shepherds, and I wanted a second chance to get it right. The fact that D had agreed to drive for hours after work showed how eager he was to welcome a large-breed canine into his life once again, too.

Sandy hair grazing the roof of the car and knees nearly bumping against the radio, he filled the small sedan with his lanky body. It was dark, and he kept his eyes on the snowy road before us as he drove. Still, as we neared our destination, he said in a reassuring voice, "Just because we drove all the way here doesn't mean you have to pick a puppy if you don't meet the 'one.' Let's just go and see."

I have never experienced love at first sight with a human being before — I guard my bruised heart so as not to succumb to that — but when I walked through the breeder's door, and saw this puppy's vitality shine through his alert eyes and miniature face, I sank to the floor and gathered him up in my arms in unadulterated wonder. He gazed at me with these intent, bluish-brown puppy eyes.

Something supernatural must have happened between us, because I don't know how else to account for it. D observed us in the background while I expressed enough exuberance for both of us. After observing several minutes of snuggling that would have made for an embarrassing introduction between humans, D nodded his youthful head in approval, saying to the breeder: "That's our boy! I don't think Michelle will go home without him."

It was 2008, and our football team, the new England Patriots, had just completed a perfect 18-0 season, led by quarterback Tom Brady. Brady, I thought, would be a propitious appellation. (Of course, little did we know that the Patriots would lose to the New York Giants in a fateful Super Bowl just a few days later.)

"Do you like Brady as a name, D?"

"It's perfect."

From the moment Brady nestled in my lap and propped his silky head on my arm, we were inseparable. The breeder had encouraged us to use the crate for the ride home, but it just looked like a cage to me, so I held Brady on my lap during the lengthy drive back to Connecticut. On Brady's first night at home, D took our first family photo — my head is cut off but you can see my arms circling a very small puppy with bright eyes and folded ears. I knew that in signing the adoption papers, I was making a commitment to provide for Brady, to be responsible for his wellbeing.

Our first night together.

D thought I would be like many people who get dogs and, when the newness of having a puppy wears off, they get bored with the routine. He had never been more wrong, which he admitted, for it was about to become my greatest skill: full-time companion of Brady. He underestimated my mettle, and to be fair, I still hadn't told him my full origin story. Before Brady came home with us, I had devised an inner contract for my relationship with this young dog. It consisted of the following tenets: 1) He would be my priority and I would be with him. 2) I would respect him and protect him when he was vulnerable. 3) I would provide the best nutrition for him. 4) I would spend my last dollar on his healthcare if he became ill. 5) We would have the same standing with each other.

Animal studies scholar Donna Haraway explores what it is we humans owe the nonhuman animals we bring into our lives. This includes questions of health. In *When Species Meet*, Haraway argues: "Dogs in capitalist technoculture have acquired the 'right to health,' and the economic implications are legion."[6] Haraway asks these thorny questions, too: "How does a companion animal's human make judgments about the right time to let her dog die or, indeed to kill her dog? How much care is too much?" For me, the answer was clear from the outset: there is no such thing as too much. I had come to the same conclusion when I was a child, and I promised myself I would be by Brady's side if he ever fell ill. I would protect him as fiercely as he would have protected me.

Haraway and I reach the same conclusion on this element of responsibility: "I am convinced that [the sky is the limit approach] is actually the ethical obligation of the human who lives with a companion animal in affluent, so-called first-world circumstances."[7] Before I tucked Brady in for the night, I said: "I would go to the moon for you if I had to." I wasn't babbling clichés. I was all in.

CHAPTER THREE
GROWING PAINS

Overnight, I turned from using academic discourse to speaking an entirely new language for me: the nonsensical language of love. Even the tone of my voice changed. I went from writing about hegemony and interpellation to waking up and cooing, "Oh, you are my little love muffin; you're just a muffin of love!"

Love relegated my faculty of reason to the hinterland of my brain. I would not go anywhere unless Brady could go with me. When D left for Arizona to attend the Super Bowl, I took Brady to my office with me—then I was on the academic job market, I was serving as the director of an educational consulting firm in New Canaan—where he slept on my lap during my consultations with students applying to college. I imagine that he was a big draw. The students coming in to see me thought the tiny ball of fur curled on my lap made the tutoring more entertaining.

I took him to the market with me. I just popped him in my computer bag, and no one said a word when tiny ears flopped out of the sides and the bag moved on its own accord. When a miniature tongue started licking the wrist holding the bag, I knew we needed to head for the check-out line. On the way home, I let him sit in my lap where he never moved; he contentedly sat curled on my lap. We had entered the Miche & Brady era.

D flew back just in time for a ski trip that we had planned pre-Brady with our Australian friends Will and Prue in Stowe, Vermont. We had reservations at the historic Trapp Family Lodge where the von Trapp singers brought the sound of music from Austria. "D, I can't go without Brady," I informed him. "I'll take care of it," he promised. And I heard him on the phone: "I understand that you have a strict no-dog policy, but would you be willing to make an exception?" He somehow cajoled them into adding Brady to our reservation, and we were off on our first family ski trip. Much later, Prue said, "Michelle, you were a goner even back then. You put him in your ski jacket and took him all over Stowe with us. I never saw a puppy and a person so connected like that. You were glowing." We did glow. I frolicked with Brady in the snow, and nestled him on the floor in my ski jacket when I went to get a sports massage après-ski. His soulful eyes peered at me through the hole in the headrest with expressions that I wanted to read.

Brady: The first canine to stay at Trapp Family Lodge

His gaze reminded me of what philosopher Martin Buber states in *I and Thou:* "An animal's eyes have the power to speak a great language."[8] When Brady's eyes met mine, they showed his world to me. They danced and beamed vitality most of the time, but sometimes a dullness showed me that he was tired or was feeling sick. I tried to follow the cues his eyes gave me. I saw love in those eyes, too. Brady's love for me had no conditions, and I knew it from the first moment I saw him. He opened my heart, and there was nothing I needed to guard against when I was with him; he told me this through his gaze and his gestures. I know that some readers may be thinking that I have an impulse to anthropomorphize, but I'll come back to that later.

Anthropologist Ray Birdwhistell notes that nonverbal behavior has a grammar that can be studied like spoken language.[9] Birdwhistell's kinesic studies found that only 30 percent of verbal interactions are determined by actual words. Anthropologist Gregory Bateson goes even further than Birdwhistell, claiming, "The point is that *no* mere words exist. There are *only* words with either gesture or tone of voice or something of the sort. But, of course, gestures without words are common enough."[10] Brady and I capitalized on every opportunity to communicate through gestures and looks, because *we got to know each other*, much as humans grow in relationships with one another. I used words to accompany my gestures, but always spoke in a warm and soft tone, mimicking the way my heart felt when I was with him. And he understood the Brady-Michelle lexicon we were developing, by responding with excitement at an invitation like: "Shall we go for a walk in the woods?" We observed one another, listened to each other, and expressed ourselves as effectively as we could with the resources at hand.

Brady was charismatic, he was affectionate, but he was stubborn, and just a touch recalcitrant. I had attended puppy school with Brady, and he had been a model student. He learned the signals immediately, from "come" to "heel" and "stay." His aptitude wasn't in question. It was his independent-mindedness that was becoming a safety issue, because he chose when to follow instructions. One day he slipped out of the car onto a busy road when I opened the door and said, "stay." I couldn't uphold my end of the contract to be responsible for him. When it took five pedestrians to help me herd the pertinacious shepherd, I knew we needed help.

I didn't want to fail in my communications with him. Náhani and Greg were my role models. They were two creatures navigating the world intrepidly as companions who respected one another. They seemed to intuit one another's boundaries and needs, and they cared for one another in spite of how disparate they seemed on the exterior. How could Brady and I emulate them?

Cognizant of something being lost in translation, I brought in top animal behavior experts for one-on-one training sessions. They acted as if Brady was a beast that needed to be tamed. His character didn't seem to factor into their regimens. D and I kept going to classes together, and Brady kept following the commands like a model student while he was showing off in class, but he continued to be stubborn at home. I knew from the story of Gregory Tah-Kloma and Náhani that if I could just access Brady's world, we could have a profound rapport. But I also knew what failure looked like.

In *Stigmata* and *Reveries of a Wild Woman*, critical theorist and writer—and my former professor in Paris— Hélène Cixous writes about the failed relationship she had with her childhood dog Fips. As a child, Cixous personified Fips as a human baby. It's what children do. But when this young dog didn't respond as a baby would, Cixous stopped addressing him forever, as if Fips were a foreign visitor who didn't speak her language. Her father, a respected Jewish doctor, cared for Fips as he would for one of his medical patients until he died, unexpectedly. As Jewish people in Algeria the family was vulnerable, and after her father's death, they were left without protection.

Insults were hurled at them and stones thrown in their yard.

Fips went mad. He was banished from the house and sequestered in the family garden on a chain. He suffered the discrimination intended for his family, and he suffered doubly from their indifference to him. One day everything came to a head and Cixous and Fips had a scuffle. Fips bit Cixous, and she stopped associating with him permanently.

Guilt reverberates through Cixous's narrative, and she stumbles over her words: "I should have spoken to him, I should have, if I had been able to understand him but I thought him perhaps incapable of understanding for I was not capable of understanding the profound animal humanity, if I had not said to myself as we precipitately lie to ourselves, that a dog does not understand our bad complications and that he is a dog."[11] I knew I risked coming to the impasse with Brady that Fips and Cixous reached. I wanted to learn from the adult Cixous, who came to the retroactive understanding that Fips was more than just a dog. From her mistakes, I was determined to get to know Brady for who he really was. To do that, we needed to log more hours together.

I did consciously bond with Brady, for the truth is that I would rather have spent a day with Brady than be with anyone in the world. Once a week, we had at least one ideal day in which we did not leave our property, and we were synchronized. We would spend the early morning outside while I watered the rose and perennial gardens. Meanwhile, Brady chased balls and brought them back to me, pausing to jump in the spray of the garden hose. I threw the red rubber ball down into the back yard repeatedly for him, never tiring of his need to play. Then I puttered in the kitchen, grinding coffee beans and preparing our separate breakfasts. Brady didn't like to eat alone; he was a firm believer in breaking bread together. I always sat down next to him on the floor, drinking coffee and eating berries, while he ate his breakfast lying down with his front paws around his bowl. I was grateful every morning that we had another day to spend together since I was over-educated in the nature of loss; being with him, my loved one, was exactly where I wanted to be.

But I hadn't come across the magical formula of how to communicate with him as profoundly as I felt we could. I also knew just how intelligent he was and wanted to give him opportunities for advanced trainings. German shepherds are historically working dogs, so I reached out to his breeder, who ran a sophisticated training operation. *Perhaps Brady was bored?* I mused.

Always in the front row for Michelle's private cello recitals.

Chapter Four
Schutzhund and its Aftermath

I wanted Brady to be stimulated physically and intellectually. I shared Brady's growing pains with our breeder in Western New Jersey, and he urged me to enroll Brady in Schutzhund training. Schutzhund, which means 'protection dog' in German, is a sport that was developed in the early 20th century to capitalize on the 'working dog' strengths of German shepherds, including tracking, obedience, and protection. *He's not a police dog, though,* I thought. To the trainer, I said: "But I don't want Brady to engage in any protection work that's violent, because we raised him in a loving atmosphere. He's a peaceful dog." I wavered because I felt very protective of Brady; after all, that was in our contract.

The breeder assured me that the first phase focused on tracking scents and learning obedience drills. "Listen, Brady is the perfect candidate for this kind of work," he said. His argument was that since Brady was so preternaturally smart, it would be a shame for him to waste his natural instincts for herding and tracking. This got me. I was horrified to think of Brady's intelligence atrophying, and he had been so bored in the training classes we had attended together.

The thought of leaving Brady with the breeder for

two weeks to conduct this training crushed me, but I was convinced that I was doing the right thing for him.

When I dropped Brady off at the training and boarding facility, the metal cage on a concrete floor that was to be Brady's home sobered me. I had brought a fluffy dog bed, several toys, multiple bags of organic dried chicken treats, and one of my worn sweatshirts to put in his bed.

At the upscale Northwinds kennel where Brady had stayed in Bedford, New York, he had his own suite. The difference in the two abodes was as stark as the contrast between the Ritz hotel in Paris and the prison where Jean Valjean was sent for stealing bread. At Northwinds, everyone pampered him. Here, it was cold concrete for a bed.

While Brady was rigorously training for Schutzhund, D and I went to Turkey for a vacation. Every single night, whether we were in the outreaches of Cappadocia, or walking among the ruins of Ephesus, I called the breeder. "How is my best boy?" I would ask. "He's fine, but I have no idea why you keep making international calls to check on a dog." He always said that Brady was doing well, but I thought his voice sounded superficial. I was beginning to feel nervous, and that instinctual part of me—that was more animalistic the more time I spent with Brady—told me that something was awry.

I didn't give the breeder advance notice that I would be arriving early on pick-up day, and the cruel scene that I saw when I pulled into the gravel drive is in the permanent collection of images in my mind. An unknown man with a muscular build and short dark hair was holding Brady on a leash in the yard. He was beating him with an electric stick.

Brady, who always looked royal with his confident stance, was standing with his shoulders hunched down, and his ears folded down over his neck like a meek rabbit. I flew. And I screamed.

"Stop! Stop! Stop hurting him! Get away from him!"

I sprinted across the yard and threw myself between

Brady and the trainer. I bent down and picked Brady up in my arms — my right arm under his bottom and my left arm under his chest so that he was cradled in my arms.

Brady collapsed against me. He feebly licked my face, pressing his body against mine as I race walked from the yard to the car. I didn't stop and I didn't look back. I booked it out of the parking lot. I allowed him to sit on my lap across the console and passenger front seat — all 75 pounds of him pressed onto my quaking thighs — up the Jersey turnpike, across the Tappan Zee bridge, and along the final stretch of the Merritt parkway before we arrived home.

I planned to comfort Brady in his safe environment after this major trauma. Still pressed into my side, he slowly made his way up the stairs. Once inside he went straight for the corner of the living room, ears folded back, shoulders hunched down. For the first time in his life with me, he found a distant corner behind a sofa to rest.

My Brady always owned the room. Now, he couldn't even look directly into my eyes, and he showed no characteristic pride. Brady looked and acted like an abused dog.

For the next few weeks, I tried calling the breeder repeatedly. "What did you do to him? You abused him! You lied to me!" I only met an answering machine.

I cried on the phone to my dad, "Brady is lost! I don't know if he'll ever come back to himself again! He only knew love, Dad! Now he's ruined! What have I done?"

I was inconsolable, but I supported Brady through his post-traumatic stress syndrome. *You have to forgive yourself; you thought you were giving him an opportunity to do what's in his DNA,* I told myself. This time — unlike when I lost Joy due to circumstances beyond my control — I was given a second chance.

Over the following days, I stayed by Brady's side, comforting him, walking with him, nourishing him, and loving him. I lay in bed with him, singing lullabies, stroking his head and long body. "I will never let anyone hurt you again," I told him over and over again. I sobbed into his glossy fur, until I could forgive myself for not heeding my gut instinct about the breeder, for not upholding my personal commitment to keep Brady safe, and for not foreseeing this. The irony was that I was trying to recover from a childhood template to practice hard and achieve, and here I had just inflicted it on Brady.

I don't believe in regrets. I think they're futile. However, if I could change only one decision that I had made in 35 years, I would never have sent Brady to Schutzhund training.

One day, Brady brought me a ball in an initiation of toss and catch. I smiled at this breakthrough. He dropped it in my lap where I was sitting in the yard, and then he sat back on his haunches staring at it. When I tossed it to him, he pounced on it happily. He dropped it and licked my forehead, as if to say that things were better with him. Hope, and a tentative sense of glee shone through the opaque storm clouds of our summer.

I was pleased, since neuroscientists like Jaak Panksepp posit that play in canines is driven by a primary emotional system in the brain that generates "endogenous opioids" resulting in a positive emotional state.[12] In other words, seeing Brady play made me think that our therapy was working.

Dad begged me to come visit. "Janet and I want to shower Brady with affection, too. It would be therapeutic for him. Please bring him." Dad had recently remarried, and my stepmother Janet was a cheerful and warm addition to our family. She told me whenever Brady visited that he'd sit next to Dad's wheelchair every moment of the day. When she came back from a walk with him, Brady would dash back in the house searching for Dad. Dad wanted to take Brady for a ride in his handicapped van — Brady's favorite vehicle — and he felt confident that he and Janet could cheer Brady up.

Brady pranced when we arrived in Vermont. Paws jutted forward, head tilted to the side, he lifted off in his unique circular movements that seemed to mean: "I am joyfully dancing with abandon at the sight of you, Grandpa and Grandma." Dad was ecstatic to see Brady's dance. His eyes lit up like blue fountains of happiness when he saw Brady, and Janet bent her short-cropped red hair down towards his face to offer him a kiss on his forehead. In Vermont, Brady slept on their bed, and I know that they caressed him when he lay next to them that week. Brady slowly came back to me, although there were flashes of his trauma that surfaced in alarming ways.

In the 'pre-traumatic' period of his life—as I'll distinguish it—Brady received many compliments. "He is such a handsome German shepherd," people would exclaim as Brady strutted down the streets of Manhattan in rhythmic stride alongside me. When he patiently allowed me to wander the aisles in the Strand bookstore, people would say, "He is so well-mannered!" At the Northwinds kennel, the owners said, "Brady gives German shepherds a good name!" Whether we encountered Danes, poodles, Labradors, or dogs of all sizes romping off the leash on the hiking trails in Mianus forest, their companions would remark, "He is so gentle with the other dogs!" These comments were universal until the fateful summer of Schutzhund training.

Something unpredictable and dark entered our lives after that. Instead of wagging his tail in his sleep as he frequently did, Brady whimpered and moaned. Sometimes, his violent nightmares included a wild thrashing of his legs and paws, and a shaking that was unbearable to witness.

Brady showed signs of aggression for the first time in his life. It became clear that he had developed a fear of certain men with medium builds and dark hair, because he lunged towards a couple of them with an alarming growl emanating from his throat.

At the end of the day, he always found his way to my pillow for our nightly snuggle session. The dark thread of unpredictability was embroidering an errant stitch in our lives, though.

Chapter Five
My Special Obligation

In August of 2009, when Brady was a year and a half old, we left Connecticut in my densely packed vehicle bound for Wisconsin, where I would be starting a tenure-track assistant professorship at the University of Wisconsin - Stevens Point. I had purchased our brick gingerbread home with a fenced-in back yard on the internet — sight unseen — on an historic street in town. We took long walks along the Wisconsin River, and hiked in the stately Wisconsin forests. Tracing the steps that my environmental hero Aldo Leopold had once taken, I wished that Mom could have joined us. As I was thinking that, my photogenic ham posed for the camera as if to break the seriousness of my thoughts. Brady sat in front of a hollow tree and cocked his head. He caught my eye with a playful regard and sat in a regal upright position, as if to say, "Won't you take a photo of me in this spot? Let me make you laugh!" I did, of course, and that photo is one of my favorites. Those moments were among our happiest since free time was scarce.

Hiking with Photogenic Brady in Wisconsin

I had so many teaching responsibilities that I would come home from campus, take an expectant Brady for a walk, grade papers, prepare lectures, and collapse around 1:00 a.m. At 6:30 a.m. the alarm would rouse us, and I would begin the process over once again. This was very different from the happy-go-lucky routine of walking, writing, walking, and writing that Brady and I had known during the first year of his life when I was on the academic job market, and could be with him at all times.

I enjoyed my students and the seminars I taught, the contemporary French film festival that I chaired, playing alto in the faculty saxophone quartet, and hilarious game nights with new friends. But a cloudiness kept settling into my brain and it was interfering with my intensive workload. Everything was taking me longer, and I didn't know why. It was similar to the mysterious condition that had affected me at Johns Hopkins, when it felt as if my brain wasn't functioning at its norm. I had chosen to teach a challenging senior seminar in French on the *Nouveau Roman*, and I am still too embarrassed to confess how many hours I devoted to class preparation.

Meanwhile, Brady was still showing signs of alarming behavior around men that resembled his abusive trainer. Around dogs, his behavior was stranger still. Sometimes he would try to hide between my legs if a large dog ran up to us on the walking trails. To my dismay, he got into a couple of scuffles with random dogs on the trails that hadn't shown the slightest signs of being antagonistic towards him. The tussles ended up harmless but were alarming all the same. And then by contrast, when my fellow professors came over to the house for Friday night games of Scrabble, charades, and merriment, Brady would smile at them with his friendly eyes, like a good host. He frolicked around them, played fetch, and rolled over on his back for belly rubs. Between my lack of energy and his odd bouts of aggression, neither of us was acting exactly like ourself.

Then, late one December night while I was grading papers, Brady collapsed. He started licking everything in sight obsessively, including a lock of my hair that he chomped off while trying to bite the air. Since he couldn't stand up, I picked him up in my arms and carried him to the car. I had saved the address for the emergency vet into my GPS system, at a fellow professor's suggestion that I remain grateful for. I drove 30 miles to the hospital at a brisk clip with snow swirling in my headlights, as I whispered reassuring words to Brady; "I promise to take care of you. I'll be right there with you." In the back seat, he was silent and immobile.

I careened into the parking lot, jumped out, and carried Brady into the hospital to place him in the vet tech's arms. My chest was palpitating wildly, and in my shock, I could feel how far away I was from family and familiarity. I watched families sobbing over animals tragically lost in what I presume to have been accidents.

The vet came out to say that Brady's stomach had begun to bloat. "Stomach bloat is the leading cause of death in barrel-chested dogs like German shepherds, so we have to operate immediately to save his life," he urged. But I would have to pay in advance before they would operate. I quickly handed over my American Express card to keep my commitment to save Brady's life. I could hear myself telling him when he was a puppy: *I will provide for you to the best of my ability.* This was our agreement, and one that I would honor at any cost.

The veterinarian came back out to discuss the surgery with me, ending our conversation with: "I encourage you to go home and come back in the morning because this is a complicated surgery." I shook my head, saying, "I'm not going anywhere when Brady's life is at stake. I'll be right here. If anything changes, please come get me." I spent the entire night shifting into various seated positions in the waiting room, trying to mold my body around the wooden contours of the chair in a comforting way to no avail. I pulled my hoodie up over my head and tried closing my eyes. I vacillated for hours—hours that seemed like caricatures, like the distance between each hour on the clock was stretched out taut—between obsessive fretting and yogic breathing to send the tension out of my shoulders, but this was a tortured meditation.

The vet came back at 4:00 a.m.

"Brady survived the surgery," he said.

We sighed together in unison, as he brushed his hand through chocolate-lab-colored hair. "We had to tack his stomach down to prevent bloat from happening again, but he made it. He's just resting until he wakes up from the anesthesia," he explained.

Years of weight slipped off my shoulders, like I had been able to help Brady when I couldn't help Mom and Joy.

"He's my life. You can't know how grateful I am to you," I rambled. Tears clogged my vocal cords, and drenched my cheeks.

At that point, I did go home to sleep for a couple of hours before teaching my 9:00 French class. My students had never seen me so pallid before, and that week they brought me "get well, Brady" gifts. The most touching gift was from a shy girl with long red hair and kind green eyes who sat in the back row. She gave me a finely crafted German shepherd Christmas ornament made out of pottery, painted with black and tan markings reminiscent of Brady's. It still sits on my dressing table as a reminder of my students' compassion for my bond with Brady, who they had seen walking through campus and town with me many times.

I raced from campus to the hospital and back twice a day that week to visit Brady as he continued to recover. When the vet told me Brady could come home a couple of days earlier than anticipated, I twirled. When they brought Brady out with his Elizabethan collar, his fragility brought my twirling to a stop. There was a long row of steel staples in his shaved stomach that I was to keep clean.

"We've got this," I told him with timid bravado.

Once we were home, I dragged my mattress downstairs so I'd be able to sleep on the floor with Brady. I didn't want to risk carrying him and aggravating the intimidating line of sutures. Brady beamed his eyes at me. He kept licking my face in appreciation, and he snuggled very closely that week as he rested from his life-threatening ordeal. I held him all night long for the first few nights, singing, "It's going to be okay, Brady is okay," even if it meant that I didn't get much sleep during finals week.

By the time Brady and I walked into the Chicago airport on our road trip home for Christmas to pick up D— who had only flown in to drive us back—we had made it through what I hoped would be Brady's last emergency.

Chapter Six
Has Anyone Seen Brady?

Summer came, and I was flattened from my year of teaching. D flew out to drive us home from Wisconsin. It was not a jubilant trip. The whole ride I felt as if my tail were between my legs. I knew something was wrong with me, but I didn't know what it was. I couldn't imagine explaining the clouds in my brain and persistent fatigue to my department chair. So, in my pride and incertitude, instead of asking for medical leave from the University of Wisconsin, I resigned from my dream job, the one that had taken 12 years of study to qualify for. I shifted around the passenger seat, unable to find the comfortable spot, the side of the highway whisking by. I was dejected and ailing in body and mind. I thought perhaps the commute was tiring me out, so I hoped to rest that summer and look for another teaching job close to home. I didn't take my symptoms seriously, and decided to focus on Brady's plight instead.

Although Brady had healed well, his erratic episodes of aggression continued to worry me. I was determined to help him regain his equilibrium, even if I couldn't find my own. I tracked down the most respected animal behaviorist in Connecticut, Chris Onthank, when we returned home the following summer. Although Chris was in high demand, he made time to work with us. I wrote him a letter explaining our intricate case. He was touched by the story of Brady's trauma at the hands of the breeder — a man he knew but whose methods he had long disapproved — and he heard the anguish in my voice during our initial consultation. Brady liked the leonine man with long blond hair who greeted us with an affable smile every week, and he clearly enjoyed that the work was done at home. There was no threat of being left in a stark place.

Chris taught me to be an Alpha when necessary, so that Brady would listen to me instead of engaging in aberrant behavior. "Meesh [he drew out my nickname], to discourage unacceptable behaviors you have to use a guttural tone that sounds like a mother dog, and lean into him, like this." Chris would tip forward and say "uh huh" in a tone that made me jump. My voice can hardly be characterized as guttural. Strangers respond to my greeting on the phone with: "Is your mother available?" Chris laughed at first, since we had become fast friends, saying, "Your years of practicing yoga and being a vegetarian took root. You have ahimsa down. But we need to ramp up your Alpha game." Once Chris was able to train me, Brady seemed to settle down under the tutelage of our skilled behaviorist. Chris took us on long walks in the woods to practice encountering dogs and people, and Brady learned how to keep a boundary. "Chris, you're a genius. I don't know what Brady and I would have done without you," I kept telling him.

Chris helped us keep our freedom within reason, too. We had installed an invisible fence so that Brady could roam freely over the several acres that we had. After a few sessions of Chris guiding Brady through the process of learning his limits, Brady was a free dog. Chris even taught him a trick using just those words. He would ask Brady to sit, then he'd throw the ball all the way across the backyard — like Brady's eponymous quarterback might have — and then let Brady loose once the ball had fallen, crying out: "Free dog!" Off Brady would race, streaking across the yard, looking like a professional athlete.

But then I lost Brady one warm day in spring when his nose carried him beyond the boundaries of our land. It was March, and I'd recently returned from leading my University of Wisconsin's study-abroad trip to Paris. When I had resigned, I had promised to still lead that winter trip. My students were excited to both see me again and France for the first time. When I returned a few weeks later, I found the pool house at our house had collapsed in an ice storm. What I didn't realize was that it would change the property boundaries for Brady's invisible fence. There was now a 25-foot space in between the flags and sensors that beeped when he was over the property limit, so he could slip through without being alerted to his unsuspecting error.

I had been engrossed in editing an academic article that was to be published (on the animal-human relationship no less), when I realized that Brady wasn't sitting in his usual spot outside by the door; he had never once strayed before. Dressed in editing attire — wool sweater, rumpled mini-skirt over leggings with wool socks, Birkenstocks, a bun on top of my head, and dark plastic spectacles — I ran through the woods and streets shrieking "Brady!" until I had unintentionally gathered a Brady-seeking posse in the neighborhood. In one of my circles back home to see if Brady had returned, I grabbed my cell phone to call D, shouting: "Brady is lost!" D told me later that he raced out of his office so fast he left the phone line dangling over the edge of his desk.

We drove through the streets in the black of the night in separate cars to cover more ground. "Braaaaady!" I called until my voice sounded like I had swallowed sawdust. I wasn't going to give up until I found Brady, even if it meant days and nights of searching. *You're doing this for Joy, too. Through thick and thin, that was the promise*, I thought.

My phone vibrated on my lap as I drove, and when I took the call, I heard one of the devoted neighbors shouting excitedly: "I've got Brady! Meet me by the Old Long Ridge fire station!" I raced along the windy back roads where I found my dog in good hands with neighbors who had offered to take care of him after a teenage boy had dropped him off at the fire station. My neighbor hugged me with a look of ecstasy on her face. I clapped my hands at her altruism. *She knows what a dog is,* I thought.

The young man had found him walking slowly along the side of my road, not at all far from my house. He put Brady in his Jeep, called his mom for advice, and upon her guidance, took him to the fire station. A neighbor was at the fire station at the time, and offered to bring Brady to her house. Why no one called Brady's vet — given that Brady was wearing Smith Ridge Vet tags — I will never know. Brady had been playing in a fenced-in yard with dogs and children for hours. He had even eaten a nice dinner while I was out searching for him frantically. Brady looked relaxed when I picked him up, whereas I was trembling. We didn't go out of each other's sight for many weeks after that incident. He wouldn't even stay outside by himself without me, trotting inside as soon as he took care of his bodily needs.

I threw a party for the whole neighborhood to thank them for helping me find Brady, and many neighbors brought gifts for Brady to my surprise. There was a joy humming all through my house as I observed people chatting over wine and conversation (mostly about animals, to my delight). *People do understand the human and animal bond,* I thought. Otherwise, they wouldn't have come out that night to celebrate the return of my beloved lupine-like dog. But it shouldn't have surprised me that this was a bond we had in common. After all, humans and dogs had been sheltering together for centuries, and humans have long fought to save their dogs, as the touching story about the Bonn-Oberkasseldog shows.

Archeologists found a dog that was buried with two humans in the same grave from 14,000 years ago in the Late Pleistocene era, which they argued demonstrated the early emotional connection between dogs and humans. Furthermore, the dog was a late juvenile with oral cavity lesions that indicated it had suffered a canine distemper infection for weeks. The team of archaeologists determined that the dog could not have survived for so long without human help. The dog was so ill that it couldn't have been of help to the humans; therefore, their care for the dog was for emotional rather than practical reasons.

In his book on canine evolution, Mark Derr suggests that wolves and humans were drawn to one another because of their social natures and their inherent curiosity. As hunters, they stayed together and reaped reciprocal benefits such as helping one another find food and providing a warm hearth. Derr proposes that wolves evolved into dogs to become part of the social structure of human and animal families: "Both human and wolf recognized at some primal level that they belonged together."[13] It was a belief I shared in, one that Náhani and Tah-Kloma had instilled in my mind as a child. Since then, too, I'd grown to know first-hand what it meant to belong with a dog. Maybe it accounted for my neighbors forming a grassroots posse to find Brady, one that took them from their own dogs and families well into the evening?

For childish reasons, I wanted to believe the debatable story that German shepherds had descended from wolves. Based on extensive genome sequencing, dogs and gray wolves can be traced to an extinct wolf lineage that disappeared thousands of years ago. The genetic history of canine domestication shows that dogs and wolves diverged about 15,000 years ago, though.

There's a lot of speculation among scientists as to how the dog evolved from the extinct line of Middle Eastern wolves, but in 2010, Robert K. Wayne, a scientist specializing in evolutionary biology at UCLA, conducted an extensive scan of DNA and chromosomes of over

900 domestic dogs and over 200 gray wolves. Wayne reached the conclusion that Middle Eastern wolves are the dominant source for genetic diversity in dogs. In 2017, Krishna Veeramah, a scientist at Stony Brook University, determined that dogs domesticated from wolves between 20,000 and 40,000 years ago.

Although the canine's closest genetic clade is the gray wolf, numerous studies (including Veeramah's) attempting to pinpoint the timing and circumstances around wolves entangling genetically to domesticate dogs are all inconclusive. Furthermore, the details surrounding dog's evolutionary narrative are murky—even among geneticists, paleontologists, and biologists.

But Brady descended from a line of working dogs that exceled at tracking, a skill Chris was teaching him the kind way, so where did Brady come from? We owe credit for the existence of German shepherds to Max von Stephanitz, a former member of the Phylax Society in Germany whose mission it was to standardize breeds. In 1899, von Stephanitz spotted a fine example of a working dog at a show, which he adopted and dubbed Horand von Grafath. Von Grafath has the distinction of being the first German shepherd dog, and von Stephanitz marked the occasion by founding the Verein für Deutsche Schäferhunde, or Society for German Shepherd Dogs. It was von Grafath's strength, build, loyalty, beauty, and intelligence that attracted the breeder. Von Stephanitz bred those traits into subsequent German shepherds that he trained for herding and shepherding (that have now, sadly, been overbred).

In keeping with his genetic inheritance, Brady responded to German, thanks to his extensive training in Schutzhund, taken over by gentle Chris. Brady would not be impressed with the imperative: "Lie down!" but he responded beautifully to Chris's German command "Platz!" When I used the word "FuB," (pronounced 'foose' for 'heel') as Chris taught us, Brady walked in alignment with me on my left side. In the event that someone approached our front door without notice, Brady refrained from barking aggressively when I shouted "Pfui!" (*fooey*). When I spoke German with Brady it meant serious business, and this was explicitly understood by both of us. After Chris trained him, von Stephanitz would have admitted Brady to the Society for German Shepherd Dogs. We had come a long way.

In spite of the scientific ambiguity I encountered when I attempted to validate a clear lupine lineage in the German shepherd, I remained fascinated with Brady's tall pointed ears and large head, his long back, and his stately stature. No matter the differences in their genetics, I had found my Náhani.

But all the sophisticated training with my bilingual dog didn't satiate my desire to communicate with him on a more profound level. Brady's expressive gaze and complex gestures made me want to learn his language, to tune into his frequency. My love for him drew me to yet another way of locating him if we were parted again: the language of Dog. It was a language he would have to help me learn. It was time to journey to the far reaches of possibility in our burgeoning interspecies relationship.

CHAPTER SEVEN
LEARNING TO SPEAK DOG

Humans have longed to converse with nonhuman animals audibly as long as they have been bonding with them. Tolstoy wrote a very convincing story, "Kholstomeer," from the animal's perspective, as if the old gelding named Strider could speak and give voice to his inner thoughts in a first-person narrative. *If Tolstoy can translate the animal's voice, then perhaps we can, too,* I thought.

This chapter is difficult to write, for I squirm in my seat knowing that the reader might be a skeptic who considers the concept of telepathic communication between animals and humans preposterous. I anticipate this as I once felt the same way. Yet even then there was a tentative curiosity to my distaste. I was someone who loved nonhuman animals and was intellectually curious. If you find yourself in the same position: I share this with you.

When an acquaintance first introduced me to the concept of animal telepathy, I cast it aside as pure hoax. When she told me of the extraordinary revelations and behavioral changes in her nonhuman animal companions, as a result of connecting with them telepathically through a famous animal communicator, I vacillated between curiosity and skepticism for a few months. Sheepishly,

I asked for the communicator's contact information. Meanwhile, I did a little research on the legitimacy (or lack thereof) of telepathy.

The word 'telepathy' comes from the Greek terms '*tele*' or 'distant,' and '*pathe*,' or 'emotion,' so as to convey an emotion from a distance; this is precisely what Brady did fluently. English Classicist and founder of the Society for Psychical Research, Fredric W.H. Myers coined the term 'telepathy' in 1882 to replace the unwieldy terms 'thought-transference' and 'thought-reading.' Myers stipulated that the term referred to both thought transference between distant persons, and to the energetic transference of emotions and sensory perceptions. This would suggest that emotions could be communicated telepathically. Telepathy was once the topic of serious scholarly inquiry for prominent philosophers and psychologists including William James, Carl Jung, and Jean-Martin Charcot. However, contemporary scholars shy away from conducting research on telepathy. I would like to suggest that it is a topic worthy of scholarly inquiry.

William James lends credibility to the subject as few could. James was a professor at Harvard University from 1873 to 1907, bridging the humanities and sciences by teaching physiology, biology, experimental psychology, and philosophy. It is well known that James has been dubbed the father of American philosophy. Less known is that James was also a founder and president of the American Society for Psychical Research in Manhattan. James, the pragmatist who sought practical solutions to philosophical problems, conducted extensive research on telepathy. I spent several days perusing the ASPR archives in the Upper West Side. James argued that an extended empirical investigation in psychical research would validate the concept of telepathy. He wrote in August 1892, "I find myself also suspecting that the thought-transference experiments […] are the sorts of thing which with the years will tend to establish themselves."[14]

Little did James know that thought-transference experiments would be conducted empirically between animals and humans in the twenty-first century, but he would have welcomed that. "Science, so far as science denies such exceptional facts, lies prostrate in the dust for me, and the most urgent intellectual need which I feel at present is that science be built up again in a form in which such facts shall have a positive place."[15] James staked his reputation as a Harvard professor to bring legitimacy to psychical research.

In my academic writing on the rapport between humans and nonhuman animals, I never thought to address the topic of telepathic communication, because even though philosophy has made inroads in rethinking the traditional animal human hierarchy, it hasn't incorporated telepathy by any means. Based on my series of irrefutable conversations with Brady, though, I can no longer avert the subject.

In spite of my mortification at the thought of being caught contacting an animal communicator, I made an appointment with Debbie McGillivray. She has written three books on animal communication, including *Untamed Voices* and *Animal Communication Bootcamp*. "I feel very blessed to be able to bridge the gap between animals and humans [...] It is through this subtle communication that questions are answered, compromise is achieved, and harmony restored," she writes on her website. In the testimonials I read, numerous clients described themselves as reformed skeptics, and thanked Debbie for the transformative changes in their animals from behavioral modifications to medical revelations. If anyone was a legitimate animal communicator, it was her.

At the appointed time one sunny early August day, I called Debbie with my list of questions that she would pose to Brady, who was sitting next to my desk. I could hear unmistakable Bostonian inflections in her voice as she explained: "I'll translate Brady's answers for you, using the tone of his energy in my vocal inflections."

51

We didn't discuss anything about Brady, about me, or about our circumstances. "What's his name, breed, gender, and geographical location?" Debbie asked me. And then, with that information, she said: "Just wait as I locate him for you."

"He has an effervescent enthusiasm." Debbie's voice was upbeat and her tone was down to earth. After admiring his physical appearance and his shining eyes, she conducted a body scan. "His right hip is sore, and his lower lumbar is out at about the fourth disk from the bottom. Can you take him to see a chiropractor?" I took notes as she spoke.

I then asked Debbie to relay several messages to Brady. I told him that he would not have to move again after our transition from Wisconsin to Connecticut. He told her that he already knew this, and he proceeded to show her a picture of our property in Connecticut. "Michelle tells me a lot of things," he explained. As I have come to learn under Debbie's tutelage, one way that nonhuman animals communicate is through sending visual pictures to her. Debbie told me that Brady was very proud of his expansive grounds, and that he particularly enjoyed swimming there.

This was an understatement, since Brady raced all the way to the pool whenever I opened the door in the summer. Most German shepherds have an aversion to water, as Joy did, so it was not as if Debbie was speaking with a breed known for its affinity for water. The images that Debbie received from Brady corresponded to our property — from the koi pond that he traipsed through when I wasn't looking, to the large pond where he swam at his own risk against my warnings about snapping turtles, and finally to the Gunite saltwater pool where we swam laps together.

When I asked simple questions such as: "Why does he resist climbing the stairs at our retreat in the Berkshires?" she responded that one time he had fallen while racing down the slippery stairs, and that he had splayed out on the bottom steps in a great deal of pain. Our steps in the

Berkshires are quite slippery, so although I had never witnessed this, it wasn't implausible. I told Brady that I would have carpet installed on the stairs for him.

When I asked if Brady had any questions for me, he told Debbie: "I'm very worried about her because she has seemed weak and depressed since we returned from Wisconsin." I confessed that I had been sad about resigning from my tenure-track job as a professor, and that I had come down with an undiagnosed illness with many debilitating symptoms, that I didn't yet know the cause of. I promised to be more cheerful for his sake.

As we concluded the 30-minute conversation, Debbie said that Brady communicated a strong love for me. "Please tell him that I love him infinitely," I gushed. I thanked Brady and Debbie profusely. I sat in a state of quasi-contentedness and quasi-stupefaction after I put the phone down. This was to be the first of many, many conversations with Debbie, our communicator and teacher who would also become our friend. I was eager to learn more.

Later that day, I made an appointment for the first time with an animal chiropractor at Rippowam Animal Hospital. I didn't tell her what Debbie had diagnosed, but when we got there, the chiropractor scanned Brady and said: "His right hip is out, and his lower disks are out." I stared at her as if she had said that I had been born on Saturn. This was a revolutionary discovery. It legitimized the intangible science of animal communication, because the veterinarian's observations corroborated with the communicator's intangible ones. I realized that the potential for communication between animals and humans was largely untapped. I couldn't wait to learn all I could from history's exchanges between animals and humans, and the technique of communicating from Debbie. Ever the academic, I went for the doctorate in animal communication.

Michel de Montaigne granted more credence to nonhuman animal's faculty of speech than any philosopher has in the past 300 years. He responds to his own question, "In how many ways do we speak to our dogs?" with the emphatic statement: "*And they respond to us.*"[16] Ascribing the faculty of speech to dogs was a radical gesture in the 1500s, and it remains to be so in 2021, but Montaigne was disdainful about human's arrogance towards animals. Debbie reminds her students, "If you listen, they will speak." She insists that her ability is the result of practice, and that we all have the ability. "Animal communication is like developing muscle, the more we build it through repetitive exercise, the more readily we can flex it when needed," Debbie explains. "The logical mind will try to override the energetic transmission, but if we put it aside, the answers will come from the animals." I read this to mean that we need to build our faculty of intuition. We just have to listen, like 16th-century humanist skeptic Montaigne was willing to do.

To communicate is to convey, transmit, and impart, and Brady and I have communicated through the five senses readily — as I've described — but if I had left it at that, I would have missed out on an entire world, his world. This is where the controversial sixth sense entered our lives.

According to the *Oxford English Dictionary*, the sixth sense is defined as: "A supposed intuitive faculty by which a person or animal perceives facts and regulates action without the direct use of any of the five senses." Everyone from Aristotle to Foucault has tried to define the ungraspable sixth sense, the *sensus communis*, or common sense, yet they all struggle because it's outside the grasp of the rational mind. To understand the sixth sense, or the intuitive sense, is to be using it.

Brady had sophisticated messages to convey through the sixth sense, and he seemed to understand what I was thinking, effortlessly. The onus was on me to build this muscle, and I couldn't rely on all the languages I had learned thus far in my academic career.

The word 'language' derives from the French for tongue, *la langue*, thus it implies an ability to speak audibly. Why, though, does it need to be audible to be legitimate? I now turn to Brady's voice to share the animal perspective on communication, since he agreed to participate in the writing of this book.

Brady was eager to respond. "Humans get so caught up in verbal communication, which is the most untrue form of communication. A human can say anything without meaning it," Brady argued. He showed Debbie a picture of a vet giving false hope to a dog's human, to show that when the vet says something untrue, her energy changes and becomes heavier. According to Brady, "Telepathy and body language—the language of animals—has to be true otherwise it won't come through." In other words, it is telepathically impossible to lie. This is in keeping with the original Greek meaning of telepathy as a way to communicate emotion. Furthermore, Brady seems to be derisive of the charade of pretending to think or feel something you don't.

We humans edit our thoughts before we speak them; nonhuman animals do not. French psychoanalyst Jacques Lacan suggests that animals are lacking in human subjectivity because they're unable to pretend or cover their tracks; for him the incapacity to feign their feelings differentiates animals from humans who have the power and consciousness to deceive. Can you imagine if humans communicated solely through telepathy? There would be no deceit or insincerity because falsehoods are impossible to convey. Philosopher Mark Rowlands writes about this topic in *The Philosopher and the Wolf* from the perspective of one who has lived intimately with a wolf. Rowlands states that a wolf cannot lie, and neither can a dog, and that's why humans are disposed to think that they are better than animals.

But I didn't want to dwell on the purported hierarchy between animals and humans, I wanted to learn how to speak Dog. I enrolled in a home-study course on animal communication that Debbie offered. First, she taught me to engage in a series of grounding exercises that enabled me to tune out static in my thoughts. From there, I was to state my intention to speak to a certain animal, ask permission to converse, and then wait for them to respond. This is a subtle process; it's almost like meditating.

I would sometimes taste things that Brady and other animals were communicating, such as the carrots that a particular horse in Vermont told me that he missed being given. I saw images, and I even felt certain sensations in my body when animals sent me messages about their physical ailments. The more I listened beyond the scope of the five senses, the more I heard profound messages. I always thanked animals for sharing with me at the conclusion of each connection, as Debbie taught me.

The first time that I tried communicating with Brady through Debbie's techniques, I was away in the Berkshires in 2011 to check on the progress of renovations there while Brady was in Vermont with my dad and Janet. I missed him, and I was eager to hear his voice with my latent senses.

When I set the intention to speak with Brady, and I called his name, I had the sensation of him wildly licking my cheeks, forehead, and nose in a nearly tangible telepathic greeting. I had a vivid image of him lying in his dog bed on top of my powder-blue ski jacket. I heard the exact words: "How many more night-time sleeps until you come?" I realized that he was distinguishing between night sleep to mark a full day, and daytime naps, to measure time.

Brady then showed me a mountain of food. I felt a full sensation in my stomach, and I felt like he was being force-fed, like a goose being prepared to become *foie gras*. My ability to sustain the connection waned quickly given my inexperience, but I felt the warmth of his love disseminate through me as I thanked him for communicating with me.

What did it all mean? I was eager to verify the images that I had received from Brady, to dispel any last vestiges of skepticism. I wanted to either confirm or not what was happening. I called my father to ask a few pertinent questions about my ski jacket and this mountain of food. Dad confirmed that when the coat closet was open that morning, Brady took the sleeve of my powder-blue ski jacket down from the closet with his teeth, gently dragged it onto his bed, and lay down on top of it. Since Brady had not placed my jacket on his bed before, Dad's anecdote reassured me of the credibility of my interaction with Brady, but I still had to ask about the food.

"Um, how much are you feeding him, Dad?" I asked, suspicious.

"Well," he said in a drawn-out way, his authoritative lawyer's voice sounding sheepish.

"I coaxed Janet into giving Brady an extra meal every day. He was looking rather thin," he said. Dad confessed that he had convinced Janet to get on the floor and spoon-feed Brady until he consumed every last morsel of raw lamb, or whatever Brady's *repas du jour* was.

"Dad!"

"Well, I didn't know I would get caught."

At that astounding point in this unusual conversation, I couldn't decide whether to feel indignant about Dad's admission, or be excited about my breakthrough. Meanwhile, Dad asked incessant questions. "How did you know that? We haven't talked about these things with anyone! Have you installed surveillance cameras in the house?"

Dad the skeptic swiftly transformed into Dad the advocate for animal communication when I explained how he had been found out.

Diffident about my skills, I often checked in with Debbie after my conversations with Brady. I avoided sharing Brady's answers with her to make sure that I was on the right track, so I would pose the same questions to Debbie that I had posed to Brady. One day she laughed and told me that Brady was bored because I had already asked these questions, but what he really wanted to know was when we were going to Vermont to see Grandpa and Grandma!

One form of communication that Brady did not appreciate was Skyping. We learned this when I left Brady with Dad and Janet for over a month while I was in Istanbul the next year for academic work. The first time that I called my father on Skype, Dad encouraged Brady to say "hello to Michelle." Brady appeared within the frame of the Skype screen, and tilted his head to and fro looking for me.

When Brady heard my voice, he became anxious and barked, panted, and paced. Dad quickly ended the Skype conversation, concerned that he had upset Brady. Dad would never have done anything to upset Brady, having repeated several times, "Our relationship with Brady is like the relationship we would have with a child. We love Brady. It's a total joy when he comes to see us." After the Skype call, Brady lay down under Dad's computer, looking despondent, until Janet convinced him to go splashing in the kiddie pool she had set up for him.

I understand why Brady didn't like Skype. It's deceitful. The sound of my voice and the image of my face were playing tricks on Brady, and he didn't like to be duped. Remember Brady's comment about the vets' energy growing heavy when they lied? My presence on the screen is an image, a copy of the authentic being, and Brady was opposed to simulacrums. He liked the real deal. Skype reminded him of his lost object — me — and threw him into a fleeting state of melancholia. He preferred the energetic version of Skype, the language of Dog, a language that may still be too futuristic for most of his fellow beings.

It was my father who said cryptically, "You should read about Strongheart." Strongheart, the famous German shepherd film star of the 1920s, conversed telepathically with J. Allen Boone. Boone, a journalist for the *Washington Post* with Hollywood connections, dog-sat Strongheart for an extended period. Boone writes in *Kinship with All Life*; "I had spoken to Strongheart in the kind of speech which does not have to be uttered or written, and he had replied to me in the same language. Without the exchange of a sound or gesture between us, each had perfectly understood the other."[17] Boone writes that a "two-way mental bridge" developed between him and Strongheart, which is one of the most apt descriptions I have read about learning the language of Dog.

The interactions between Boone and Strongheart would be extraordinary to most, but I felt like I was reading about my quotidian life with Brady. The book was a bestseller when it was published in the 1950s, and Harper Collins described the book as "proof that communication with animals is an indisputable fact." I only wonder why it hasn't become more commonplace to speak Dog, based on Boone's widely publicized conversations with Strongheart.

Energetic communication can only be effective with nonhuman animals as a "two-way" bridge if the human can achieve a calm state, free of distraction, and outside stimulus. We humans are perpetually overstimulated with cyber communication—text messages, social media, and emails. We have cultivated a state of distraction, so tuning into an animal's subtle frequency is challenging, and it requires patience. To chat with our animal friends, we must find our own inner quiet first; the reward of speaking with one's animal friend is well worth it.

But you can't control the content your nonhuman animal friends share, even if it's embarrassing. Although I was too humiliated to tell my friends how much my body and mind were malfunctioning, Brady told Debbie about my debilitating symptoms that cast a cloud over our joyful walks and adventures. We had finally received a diagnosis of late-stage Lyme disease, and it altered my life so much that even my ability to care for Brady was in question.

Chapter Eight
Preparations for the Storm

A couple of years passed and the peonies had made their annual return to Connecticut. I was only able to teach one class, part-time at a local university — even that was physically and intellectually overwhelming for me — and when the spring semester ended, I submitted my university students' final grades to the registrar. No one but Brady and D knew it, but efficient Professor Slater could barely make it through class, let alone driving back and forth to campus. I started making mistakes in my classes, which I taught exclusively in French, using the wrong verb tense, or forgetting completely what I was explaining. When a fellow professor stopped me in the hallway to ask what I had written my dissertation on, I couldn't remember. I clenched the steering wheel on the Merritt Parkway with stiff hands, hoping I would follow its curves and land at home where I could collapse. Brady lowered his expectations of me. Our afternoon walks were replaced by pajama parties.

To compensate for Brady's loss of exercise, D would throw red rubber balls to him across the yard every morning and night. I had taught him Chris's "free dog" trick, which D loved. He would have Brady sit for him, throw the ball with his long arm, and admire that Brady wouldn't budge until he called "free dog!" In between these romps, Brady would curl up near my failing body where he could observe both me and the door, in case anyone dared to disturb his resting girl. I wouldn't have known or cared if a thief had entered the house, I was in such a deep stupor, and he knew that. He had my back and more.

At some point during the year, Brady contracted Lyme disease, too, so we both lay miserably in bed all afternoon. Once, what with two gargantuan bottles of antibiotics in the kitchen, I accidentally took Brady's pills and gave him mine. This happened more than once as I muddled my way through the day.

When the cloud cover cleared in my brain — which it did as randomly as the clouds in the sky moved — it seemed ironic that I was learning the silent (yet nuanced) language of Dog while I was losing my own languages, French and English. I thought I was losing my mind.

To restore my loss of internal peace, my lack of confidence in my faulty brain, I went online to make summer plans. Yoga had long been my sanctuary in times of stress, so I planned to attend restorative classes at the Bedford Post just down the road from me. As I was signing up, I stumbled upon Harvard-trained psychiatrist Dr. Vijaya Nair's Introduction to Meditation class there. Dr. Nair channeled her lifelong spiritual experiences into teaching meditation and mindfulness, according to her course description.

I have been meditating since I was a teenager, but something about this class attracted me. When I arrived for the first session, Dr. Nair whirled into the room exuding peace; we were eager to hear her speak. She embraced us with her lively eyes before she launched into a plethora of facts about meditation. "Did you know that the human mind produces 70,000 thoughts per day?" She convinced us that we needed to meditate so that these thoughts did not run us wild. They had been creating havoc in me for quite some time, especially now that I couldn't remember most of them, and I was lagging in my contract to take care of Brady to the best of my ability. I perked up.

"Close your eyes and imagine breathing vibrant light into every area of your body. Now imagine sending this healing light to every human, animal, organism, and plant in the universe—even the persnickety politicians and murderers." Dr. Nair guided us as an ineffable peace wafted through my fascia muscles and between my shoulder blades. She had been trained in Transcendental Meditation, or TM, which has been proven by Harvard researchers at Massachusetts General Hospital to make significant changes in the areas of the brain associated with memory, stress, and empathy.

When I meditated with Vijaya—as she bade me to call her when I started working with her in private sessions—she used a hybrid technique unknown to me called Jyoti meditation, or light meditation. Vijaya dissolved my issues, one by one. I had had chronic insomnia with Lyme disease, but after meditating with Vijaya, I was suddenly sleeping. I would sit in my meditation chair at night and release any thoughts that weren't serving me well. Fears would surface while I was meditating, and I would acknowledge them and release them. Brady sighed by my side.

I had never been able to shake a deep sadness and residual shock about my mother's death, but suddenly I felt joy when I thought of her. To symbolize this, I planted an elaborate rose garden that summer to commemorate her—with Brady helping me dig the rose bush holes—and it thrives to this day.

Somehow, the meditation eased my Lyme pain, almost more than the antibiotics did. Or, it was simply one of the mysterious reprieves from Lyme that would come upon me, like landing on a "Get out of Jail Free" card unsuspectingly during a game of Monopoly. The effects of these meditations were transformative, as if the universe was preparing me for a great battle. I didn't know that the Grand Battle was about to start, and I would have to call on all of my valiancy to fight. I had been preparing for this since I was a child.

Chapter Nine
From a Five-Star Vacation to a Five-Star Hospital

When Brady collapsed into a lethargic heap of feverish black and cinnamon fur—looking nothing like the vivacious German shepherd I knew so well—I raced him to the emergency veterinary hospital in Norwalk, Connecticut, trying to reach the speed of light. The late summer sun bore down on us on that Sunday afternoon as I carried him to the backseat of my car. As we took off swiftly, words that I had written in my journal earlier that summer haunted my fraught mind: "My greatest fear is losing Brady."

That's right, in a time when discrimination, global warming, economic and political volatility, war, disease, and the threat of extinction confront the human and animal kingdoms, my fear was losing my closest companion on the planet. Although most strangers might not understand my fear of loss, those who knew my history with Grief would understand.

With Brady, it was as if our DNAs had been intertwined, so what happened to him happened to me. As I drove towards the vet, I felt the link between us tauten in my body, not wanting to prophesy the harrowing experience that could come, not wanting to catapult us into any more medical emergencies, wanting to seize our peace and hold onto it.

When we came to a rare stretch of the historic tree-lined Merritt parkway with little traffic, I twisted my head around to see how Brady was holding up. We only had a nanosecond to talk when my bright hazel eyes met his forlorn chocolatey ones. "We are going to the doctor," I said in a reassuring tone. It was one of the many phrases in our Brady-Michelle lexicon, and he sighed in acknowledgement.

We had just come from a matchless holiday in late August. To reward him for his patience all semester, I had wanted to take Brady on a summer vacation where we would engage in activities that would interest him. This meant swimming. Brady's vacation was perfect from his perspective, for he was swimming every day for a week in sunny Vermont with his girl. We swam in timeworn swimming holes carved by rock canyons in the Mad River near Waitsfield. In Stowe, we walked deep into the forest to frolic in the fairy-like Moss Glen Falls where pine needles liberally coat the forest floor, moss embroiders itself on rocks, and a canopy of coniferous trees form the frame for gradated falls. We spent the entire day there picnicking and swimming in the hidden sanctuary that has a Tolkien-like quality.

We drove all the way to Lake Willoughby one day, in the remote Northeast Kingdom, a landscape formed by glaciers and surrounded by rocky hills. Brady swam in the sparsely populated pristine waters, free from algae and muck, right next to the "No dogs allowed at the beach" sign. I threw sticks and Brady paddled to catch them in his mouth, while I clapped and cheered him on.

When I joined him, we swam in a synchronized way with Brady jutting his head out, right by my side. I would keep my head out of the water, too, blond hair fastened in a messy bun on top of my head, oversized black sunglasses perched on my sunscreen-drenched nose. Brady looked content and confident when he swam next to me, as if it was his greatest pleasure.

It was just the two of us staying at my dad's empty house — Dad was in Maine and D was away on business — but we must have gone through 40 clean towels that week. My vehicle bore the aroma of wet dog and sweaty human, particularly in the two front seats where my co-pilot and I both sat on towels. We were at the pinnacle of happiness, though. For Brady, this was a five-star vacation, and any vacation spent with Brady merited five stars as far as I was concerned.

A rugged hike up Camel's Hump on the 4th of July when we were healthy.

Upon our return to Connecticut, however, Brady seemed spent, just as I was. Going into the weekend, he showed distinct signs that he wasn't feeling well, such as running away from his favorite raw meal. Brady had been on an exclusively raw food diet since he was born. I had wanted to match what ancestral dogs might have eaten: a diet of raw meat, bones, and organs, with some ground vegetables added in for good measure. On Thursday, Brady slurped water as if we had been hiking in a desert, and he pleaded to pee in the middle of the night, an anomaly for him. I didn't know what the word 'polyuric' meant then.

Early Friday night, September the 13th — not an auspicious date if one is superstitious, which I am not — I said: "Michelle goes. Brady stays." Brady sighed, clambering up on the white daybed in the foyer where he could watch both main doors in my absence. I left for Doug's 40th birthday party; he was a close childhood friend from Interlochen, one who had seen me through the gloomiest period of my life when my mom died.

I made a brief appearance at the elegant party in Tribeca, hugged old friends, and then I started to fret. "Doug, I don't want to leave Brady alone for too long because he has been feeling off," I said. "We all know how you feel about Brady. Go to him," he said with a laugh.

Brady padded to the door and leaned into me when I returned, nestling his face in my hand, but there was no enthusiastic tail wagging. I wanted to comfort him when we went to bed. My sheets had just been laundered and the bed was neatly made. I caught Brady's gaze and patted the bed. That particular night, Brady put his paws on the bed, and looked around at me, to see if I would lift his rear. Usually, he jumped up on his own accord. I lifted him up to snuggle.

Within minutes, he vomited an entire meal right on my pillow; a meal I had had to hand-feed him earlier. Murmuring "it's okay, it's all right," I lifted him up and placed him down on his own bed while I replaced the soiled sheets with fresh ones. I lifted him back up on my bed and wiped his mouth with a towel. I gently pet his head as I said: "I'll be right here with you for the rest of the weekend. Michelle stays." He nestled deeper into my shoulder, exhausted. I would have taken him to the vet immediately, but it was a weekend and our regular vet was closed.

We had a quiet day at home on Saturday. I sat close to Brady on the lawn and stroked his face. I admired the flecks of rich cinnamon, black, and fawn that weaved through the top of his head like natural highlights. I caressed the thick cream and tan swath on his cheeks that feathered into the full copper ruff that framed his face like an Elizabethan collar. I drew my hands over the black shiny fur on his back and ran them down onto his large cream paws and forelegs. *I'm so lucky I get to spend my life with my regal dream dog,* I thought with contentment. Merely being with him brought my autonomic nervous system into a peaceful place, as if I had been meditating.

"Do you want to go for a walk?" I asked on Sunday morning. Brady nudged me with his nose, and gave an affirmative bark. He ambled along the streams and forests on the bike path in Pound Ridge, New York, with curiosity and enthusiasm, as if it were a typical Sunday. I sighed in relief, and even said: "Ah, we must have just had an off tummy, right?" I knelt down and stroked his cheeks while he licked my nose in return.

But by the afternoon, when we visited my friend Jennifer, he had plummeted. He lay supine on the floor, without a trace of his normal exuberance at seeing friends. Nor did he extend his signature greeting, which consisted in laying his ears back, kissing hands, and wagging his tail with carefree abandon. When it was time to leave, he collapsed, legs splayed out. Brady had made a valiant effort to mask his illness, but Monday morning was too long to wait.

We finally arrived at the VCA hospital, located in a rundown neighborhood just off from Interstate 95 after it connects with the Merritt Parkway. I parked and staggered in with Brady in my arms.

Multiple receptionists were manning the phones and checking patients in and out. They were used to frantic, and it didn't daunt them, so they gestured for us to sit down in the waiting room where a Keurig coffee station stood. The Seattle Seahawks were walloping the New York Giants to add to the chagrin of those watching and waiting.

Some people looked like they had just come from the beach with their companion animals, sporting flip-flops and sun visors. Some sat in shock. One distinguished man sat in a suit, looking as nonchalant as his two Afghan hounds did. A mother and daughter were in tears, and I looked away from their faces to stay strong for Brady. To my surprise, the receptionists led us to a private consultation room right away. We were glad to circumvent the discomfort of the hectic reception area and acclimate to this strange new environment on our own terms.

Brady sniffed and paced the perimeter of the room. I coaxed him to lie down and rest his head on my knee by playing Kirtan musician Krishna Das on my iPhone. Krishna Das's Indian chanting always had a calming effect on us, especially as we navigated Manhattan traffic. As Krishna Das droned on about Baba Hanuman, I took a few deep breaths through my nose, and exhaled the tension in my shoulders and chest until I felt my own anxiety dissipate. Vijaya had prepped me well since the emergency surgery in Wisconsin, and I was grounded this time in the face of adversity. I couldn't fall apart for Brady.

Multiple doctors and technicians came in and out of the room wearing white coats with their names embroidered over their hearts, taking Brady's temperature, extracting blood samples, and palpitating his lymph nodes. Brady endured the prodding and poking like a stoic. We waited for several hours for results in our room. His stiff, closed mouth showed me how concerned he was, yet we exchanged feelings of reassurance and strength. We made a pact to be valiant in our inaudible language.

After several hours, Dr. Beth Whitney, one of the leading veterinarians, came in. "Brady isn't well enough to return home tonight, but we don't know the cause of his life-threatening symptoms yet," she explained. I nodded in a stupor. She went on, "His fever is 105, and that's dangerous. He'll need to spend the night here on fluid therapy and antibiotics to bring it down." I accepted the news peacefully, because I didn't want to alarm Brady with catastrophic thinking. I turned to him and said, "You are precious, and I trust these doctors to take the utmost care of you." I ended with a soft "Michelle go, puppy stay." I looked toward the vet intently as I spoke these words, and she got what the stakes were, because she nodded gravely. Dr. Whitney's assistant put Brady on their leash, and she handed his leash and collar to me for safekeeping.

This small gesture startled me more than any other. It concretized the disquieting reality that Brady was staying there without me. I suppose the equivalent would be a scenario in which my partner admitted me to the hospital, and the nurses gave him my necklace, rings, and watch when he left me there in their hands. The empty collar and Brady-less leash called out stridently: "Absence, separation."

As they led Brady away, he struggled against the foreign leash, his paw nails scratched and slid on the tiled floor, and he turned his expressive velvety eyes back toward me to lock them with mine. He was counting on me, and he let me know it. I repeated to him in my soft, sing-songy voice that was reserved just for him: "Michelle go, puppy stay. I'll be back in a little bit." Even if it was fleeting, the word 'absence' was not in our vernacular. Togetherness was our theme; that's what we did best, and it was in our contract. I continued to hear the echo of his scratching nails protesting this forced separation as I walked reluctantly to my car. The echo numbed my chest.

I couldn't go from the overstimulating hospital to overwhelming Interstate 95. The back roads of Connecticut appeal to me, so I thought of a way to cut in through the old apple farms of Norwalk and along the stolid stonewalls of New Canaan, as I meandered towards North Stamford.

The mantle of tree branches over the road were a safe haven, and I encountered no one but jaywalking squirrels. I drove all the way up my long, dark driveway, lined by tall conifers. My stone house looked foreboding in my headlights for the first time. I had never been there without Brady.

I walked through the front door and into my solitude. The house was two-dimensional without Brady. It felt more like a museum, and I felt like a visitor who was breaking the rules and staying overnight. I suddenly realized that Brady made the house come alive as if it were an animate being like the two of us. I lumbered up the dark oak stairs without saying my customary bedtime phrase to Brady, "going up." I could see Brady scampering up onto my pillow to nest, but I repeated to myself: "He won't be here tonight." My chest felt iced against the heat of the Indian summer evening.

I sighed as I installed myself in cross-legged position on the eggplant velvet chair in my bathroom to meditate. If I hadn't been meditating intensively that entire summer, I would have been in a state of panic. I knew that dogs didn't lead eternal lives, and this terrified me. I have never said to another creature, human or otherwise, "Waking up next to you is like Christmas every day!" But joy flowed through me whenever I woke up and saw Brady, and he would come to my bedside to deliver his morning greeting of two licks on the cheek. "True love is rare," I would groggily tell him as I stroked his cream velvety cheeks in return. I had always averted love, built fortress-like boundaries around my heart, and attempted to replicate the stoicism I admired in my maternal grandfather. I didn't want to meet Grief again the way I did when Mom and Joy died. But when I do love, I am rendered defenseless in my devotion. Efforts to remain stoic when it came to Brady were futile.

Vijaya would have said that I had to address my attachment issue with Brady. She would have said that I was attached to a certain outcome — one in which Brady would survive any illness. An example of attachment would be holding onto someone so fiercely that you cannot live without them. With all of this in mind on the night that Brady went to the hospital, I closed my eyes and profoundly exhaled the tension in my chest where fear was brewing.

I quietly breathed in that ephemeral state of peace I only found through meditating, allowing it to spread through my shoulders and soften them. In spite of the gravity of the situation, I was able to come to a quiet place. I brought the fear about losing Brady to my mind. I allowed it to manifest in this safe space, and I acknowledged it. When I felt the fear at its thorniest, I tried to just sit with it. I released my need to control the outcome of his illness, if only for fleeting moments. Only then was I able to go to bed alone.

When I woke up the next morning without Brady at my bedside, I dialed the emergency hospital, eager to retrieve him. The receptionist gently said: "5:00 a.m. is a touch too early." At least they knew that I was not about to abandon Brady there. When I spoke with the doctor a couple of hours later, I was crestfallen to hear that Brady's fever had not come down. We were deep in the territory of the unknown, my least favorite dwelling place.

September was a stunning month in Connecticut that year. The combination of cerulean skies and Indian summer breezes created the perfect offing for hiking in the 4,000-square-mile Ward Park Ridge reservation, where Brady and I had enjoyed many autumnal walks. Every year I looked forward to the cooler days for walking, as did Brady, since his sartorial choices in the muggy New England summers remained limited to his thick fur coat. I was woeful at the thought of Brady being stuck in the hospital, unable to go hiking with me on the random days I had a reprieve from Lyme.

When I reached the hospital and entered the lobby, they announced me on an intercom: "Brady Slater's mom is here." I waited patiently, strong as a Connecticut maple tree, until I heard the unmistakable sound of his nails creating friction on the floor as he pulled against the leash on his way to finding me. He careened towards me and I met him halfway, where I kneeled to greet him on his level. He circled me in excitement and relief. His eyes were dancing at the sight of me; he didn't look like a sick dog to me—but I frequently heard from people that I didn't look sick when I was barely standing upright.

One very nice thing about the emergency hospital is that we had a room to ourselves, albeit one that bore a pungent bleach bouquet. The doctors didn't know the cause of Brady's illness, but they still wanted to keep him on observation and fluids until the fever came down, and they had the lab work back. Brady lay down and placed his head on my lap when everyone left. I already felt the characteristic warmth spread over me that I always felt when I was in Brady's presence. "Have I told you today that I love you?" I asked him softly, knowing that I had.

Brady was unquestionably my soulmate dog, but why, you might ask, was my soul mate a dog? I've considered this often, and what I keep returning to is that something in him touched me that humans weren't able to, or maybe that I wouldn't let them. When I was a child, my parents frequently told me they loved me, and I knew they meant it. But they seemed the happiest when I showed signs of being a child prodigy as a saxophonist. D was a loyal partner, but one who sometimes spoke to me in harsh tones reminiscent of his Soviet origins. Brady didn't expect me to be a superstar. Thank goodness, because I'm not. Brady didn't growl at me upon occasion and look like he was going to bite me. Good, because I would've hidden in the closet. What Brady did have was a seemingly limitless reservoir of attention, love, respect, compassion, and kindness at his disposal. He radiated love, and it was infectious. My friends always fell in love with him at first sight. I didn't have to do anything, be anything, achieve anything to receive his love. He gave it to me freely. And I returned it. It was symbiotic, and we trusted each other enough to love like that.

I realize that many scientists and scholars would contest the possibility that Brady understood me enough to be considered my soulmate dog, and they would think I had imagined Brady's expressions and ability to return my love. As ethologists Raymond Coppinger and Mark Feinstein argue in *How Dogs Work:*

> Dog lovers love to draw rich conclusions about the minds of their animals. The notion that their pets might be 'conscious agents' with felt mental states, intentionality, and a sense of self seems to be especially appealing: countless dog owners are delighted to believe that 'Rover is happy/ sad/loves me..." [...] Much of this picture of a dog's mind, we think, is an illusion generated by our deep-seated and persistent impulse to anthropomorphize—by the fact that many of us want to believe that our close animal companions are like us and able to understand us.[18]

I acknowledge the reactions these scientists would have, deny my tendency to anthropomorphize, and choose to stick with the empirical evidence I had at hand.

I began to stroke Brady's familiar coat to comfort him in this foreign place, and he sighed and snuggled up to me even more, emanating a stress-relieving cross between a groan and a yawn. A grawn. Just by being together, my chest hummed with contentment. Brady turned his head to the side so that he could look up at me and hold my gaze, and we stared at each other in mutual adoration. Any angst I had felt on the drive to the hospital was effaced once we were physically together. This always happened, when I was anxious or worried or sad, and I'd often wondered if there was a scientific explanation for the physiological and emotional changes Brady stimulated in me. While I was anxiously absorbing all the changes brought to me life from being ill with Lyme—being told to acclimate to a new normal that felt very abnormal—a therapist even told me that I should have an emotional support dog (which I already had). Was there something scientific about that idea?

The answer involved oxytocin, dopamine, beta-endorphins, and serotonin. Oxytocin is a neurotransmitter that initiates positive physiological changes including slowing the heart, quieting blood pressure, and keeping stress hormones at bay. It creates a sense of calm and comfort. As naturalist Sy Montgomery writes, "Our pets profoundly change the biochemistry of our brains."[19] A Japanese study showed that when humans have increased levels of oxytocin, nonhuman animals were more attracted to them, licking and pawing them. Brady triggered such a high oxytocin release in me, it's no wonder that he was constantly licking my face and hands.

Montgomery reports that when humans spoke to their companion animals and petted them, "the interaction boosted levels of beta endorphins — natural painkillers associated with 'runner's high' — and dopamine, known widely as the 'reward hormone.'"[20] As if that weren't enough to convince everyone to rush out and find a dog, Montgomery cites a University of Missouri study that proves petting dogs causes serotonin levels to spike in humans. Brady and I had known this for a long time, based on our home-grown empirical experiments. I curled up on the cold tiles of the emergency hospital floor for my daily dose of dopamine, and I administered Brady's dose of neurotransmitters to him.

As the days passed, the doctors realized that Brady and I had a special bond.

"Stay as long as you like," Dr. Whitney encouraged me. I visited longer than any of their patients' families had before. It took them time in the morning to complete their rounds, take blood samples, and administer medications to all of their patients, so they asked me not to come before late morning. I arrived around 11:00 a.m. and frequently stayed until bedtime.

I would set myself up on the tattered blankets they provided us with. I practiced mindful breathing to calm both of us down, and I chatted with Brady. Brady understood so many English phrases, on top of the fluent way he communicated silently. We didn't engage in English language drills, of course, I just spoke to Brady as if I were naturally speaking to another human. "You're so brave. You're doing so well," I'd say. Then I would read, sometimes out loud to him. I brought my raw vegan "hippie salads" as my friends called them, and the inquisitive front desk receptionists would come in and chat with me about my raw vegan diet. I was becoming a regular at the emergency hospital.

Brady's charisma waned a few days into his hospital stay. When I scrutinize the photographs from that time period, it pains me to see that his trademark effervescence had gone flat. Instead of holding his shoulders back and proudly holding up his handsome head, he molded his entire body to the floor. His ever-mindful ears were pricked up because a shepherd never rests from his watchful duties, but the rest of his body reflected his depression at being sick in this sterile place.

As we hung out on the floor, we practiced what biologists call allogrooming, in which animals of the same species groom one another. Brady liked to lick the tear ducts around my eyes when I woke up in the morning, but in the long hours spent in our room at the emergency hospital, Brady licked my arms or hands, especially if I had a speck of gardening dirt on them. He liked to make sure that I was well groomed and clean, as if it were part of his duty. I cleaned the crusty bits from his tear ducts, and I wiped his ears out gingerly. He would lean into my hands as I did so, and groan mildly, as if it were pleasurable for him. I inspected his paws and wiped them, and he would even hold them up for me, assisting me in the allogrooming practice. All the time I was tending him, I kept displacing any bad news for another day.

On Wednesday afternoon Dr. Whitney came to see us. "Brady has contracted leptospirosis," she said gravely. "It causes one or more of the following: kidney failure, liver failure, heart failure, or death." After days of waiting, it hit me like a broken piece of iceberg in my chest. "Brady is experiencing acute renal failure as his primary symptom to lepto," she continued.

"He was vaccinated for lepto in Wisconsin," I protested. Tilting her blond head sympathetically, the way Brady sometimes did when he was listening, Dr. Whitney explained that "the lepto vaccination is problematic; it doesn't always work." Then, she asked the fatal question: "Was Brady swimming in any rivers or streams recently?"

Chilled by that feeling of an iceberg in my chest, I felt very sober, and numb, too. Guilt permeated my tone when I told her about our summer vacation in Vermont, and she brushed her hand through her short-cropped hair as my voice wavered. "It's not your fault," Dr. Whitney told me emphatically.

I railed against her reassuring words. Standing there it felt very much like my fault. And what irony! I enabled Brady to have the vacation of his dreams, and said vacation caused a life-threatening illness. His dream vacation was quickly becoming his bucket list vacation. The metaphorical iceberg in my chest cut me with its jagged edge when I realized that swimming in potentially contaminated waters probably caused Brady's kidney failure.

"Brady will have to stay in the hospital for an indefinite period. He'll be attached to the IV machine 24 hours a day through the catheter that we have already inserted into his vein," Dr. Whitney continued, as if I had not already been inundated with catastrophic news.

"You're at risk for catching leptospirosis because you're in such close contact with Brady. From now on, you should wear gloves and a facemask around him," she cautioned.

I was no longer processing her news, though, and I had a raging Lyme headache from concentrating on the medical details of leptospirosis. "Dr. Whitney, please give him every treatment possible. Meanwhile, I will be his moral support," I stated through the brain fog that was moving in fast. Brady was part of me. I was part of him. Guilt would not be getting me this time, like it had done with Joy.

The billing department prepared yet another estimate, and it was staggering. I signed it in a stupor, and they charged a percentage to my beleaguered American Express card, which they had on file. They had been charging it regularly thus far. No matter how expensive the bill was, I would pay it without question. I was humbled at how fortunate D and I were to be able to afford Brady's care. But what if we couldn't have paid the bill?

When Brady was eight weeks old, and he visited Smith Ridge Vet for his first check-up, I saw brochures for pet health insurance on the receptionist's counter. *After all, Brady should be covered in the event of emergencies and unforeseen health issues,* I thought. That evening, I showed them to D, but he scoffed at my idea, flashing his Slavic eyes at me, and saying: "How ridiculous can you be? These insurance companies are a scam. We would pay more in premiums throughout his lifetime than we would ever see in return."

Health insurance for dogs surely did not exist in the Soviet Union when he was growing up, and I didn't pursue it further, since we were raising Brady together. However, hypothetically, had we enrolled our young German shepherd family member in a reputable health insurance program at that time, our financial burden would have been greatly mitigated.[21] Brady's case makes the quintessential argument *for* having pet insurance.

On that inauspicious night, I logged onto my Johns Hopkins alumni library account to read everything I could glean from medical journals about the disease my canine half was battling. *Leptospira* are thin, coiled bacteria in the genus of spirochetes that derive their name from the Greek words 'leptos,' or fine, and 'spira,' or coil. Spirochetes are one of the most aggressive forms of bacteria, and they are also found in syphilis as the subspecies *Treponema pallidum,* and in Lyme disease as *Borrelia*. Some of my favorite French authors had died from syphilis, and since Brady and I had both been combatting Lyme disease, which was winning decidedly in my fight, I was already all too familiar with how pernicious the leptospira spirochetes could be.

Domestic animals contract leptospirosis primarily from rodents that are dormant carriers. However, when dogs drink water from stagnant streams, local bodies of water such as rivers, or lick the grass where infected rodents urinate, they can contract leptospirosis. I had been in such a state of delirium when Dr. Whitney had warned me that leptospirosis was a zoonotic disease, so I was alarmed to read a World Health Organization report that leptospirosis is a highly contagious disease, which means that dogs can transmit it to humans. The WHO estimates that between five and 25 percent of leptospirosis cases in humans result in death.

If I were going to contract lepto, I had already been exposed. I wasn't going to wear a mask and plastic gloves around Brady, as the vets recommended; he needed my affection and support. I refused to filter my affection through an alienating layer of plastic. Besides, I was already taking antibiotics for Lyme disease, so I couldn't possibly contract leptospirosis, I rationalized. Or, at least it couldn't be worse than my losing war with Lyme already was. I had my own aggressive spirochetes to contend with, but I was prepared to go to battle for Brady to be rid of his. What I really needed to do was become a kidney expert.

One fifth of the blood that entered Brady's circulation system during each heartbeat was routed directly to the kidneys. These two bean-shaped organs located behind his chest play a fundamental role in maintaining multiple bodily functions, including blood pressure. They produce red blood cells, hormones, and enzymes. The kidneys detoxify metabolic waste such as urea, poison, or excess mineral salts from the blood, doing just what juice fasts promise: detox.

Waste moves through the kidneys to the thousands of microscopic nephron systems, or kidney units, that filter through infinitesimal glomuleri—or kidney nerve endings—that then wash the blood, and send clean blood back towards the heart for another cycle. The leftover waste gets excreted through the urine. This intricate process illustrates just how critical the kidneys were to sustaining Brady's vitality. My ability to read and assimilate waned quickly to my dismay; the familiar brain fog of Lyme disease was settling in.

Early the next morning, (and every morning thereafter) I woke up and dialed the emergency hospital to ask for Brady's daily kidney values. Dr. Whitney—who was a kidney expert—explained that Brady's creatinine and BUN values had risen as a consequence of acute renal failure. I strained to understand the battle taking place in Brady's vulnerable body. As a literature professor, I heard the words 'acute' and 'failure' and thought they signified doom, so I was trying to overcome the anxiety they created in me by focusing on the medical facts.

Creatinine is produced as a waste product of creatine, a chemical comprised of nitrogeneous organic acid that supplies energy to all cells. The kidneys work continually to remove creatinine from the body. However, if kidney function is on the decline, then less creatinine is released through the urine, causing levels to rise. Higher values indicate various stages of kidney failure. If the kidneys and their sophisticated filtering system start to falter, toxic waste accumulates in the recirculating bloodstream. If the balance of fluids, minerals, and electrolytes is disturbed by disease, organ complications ensue. In addition to monitoring Brady's creatinine through a daily blood test, doctors were testing Brady's BUN values, otherwise known as blood urea nitrogen.

Urea is formed when protein breaks down in the body. It's manufactured in the liver and eliminated from the body through urine. The BUN test calculates the amount of nitrogen in the blood derived from urea. In Brady's case, Dr. Whitney and her team were calculating his BUN and creatinine ratio. The ratio should be between

10:1 and 20:1. An increased ratio is due to a decrease in the flow of blood to the kidneys, or what is scientifically known as renal failure.

Brady's creatinine and BUN values changed like the wind, and sometimes they spiked overnight. As a self-proclaimed budding amateur nephrologist—or kidney expert—I kept a kidney value journal next to my bed that I could easily access in the morning when I woke up and called the vet. The journal grew to have endless columns of numbers that shifted upwards and downwards with little pattern to explain them. Every morning, after the on-duty vet relayed the kidney values to me, I encouraged her to believe in Brady's recovery.

If I had not meditated, these daily blood reports would have sent me into a state of debilitating panic. The more dire Brady's report was, the more I meditated, and it not only prevented panic from forming, it built muscles of inner strength. If I wasn't strong, who would advocate for him? How would he have the wherewithal to persevere? Strength alone would not suffice. My meditation practice brought me peace. It alleviated my fears, so I could bring the necessary mental ingredients of calm *and* strength to Brady every day. It enabled me to believe in his recovery.

I created an email group called "Team Brady," comprised of those friends and family members who had reassured me that he would get better. When I sent periodic updates and requests for emotional support, Team Brady replied with encouraging messages that held me up like intangible pillars. My cousin wrote: "Good morning honey, He is a fighter and will get better, and you are the inspiration for all of us with your determination and patience. He will be fine. I am sure of this." My friend Jennifer wrote: "I will be lighting a candle for Brady tonight, and sending his sweet soul some love." Vijaya wrote: "By your brave example, I am sure we are all experiencing huge shifts in our own lives!" As my spirits started to flag, these messages encouraged me to keep fighting the battle to save Brady's life. And I talked to Debbie almost every day.

I called Dr. Mike Bartholomew at Smith Ridge Vet every few days to consult about Brady's kidney values and to get his holistic opinion. Dr. Mike had been treating Brady for a long time, and his voice over the phone was soothing. He reviewed the lab reports every week.

Brady's veterinary team wasn't so sure about his recovery, and they reiterated this time after time. Dr. Whitney supervised Brady's case diligently, and her team was constantly calculating fluid ratios. They warned me that on short notice Brady might have to be transferred to the Animal Medical Center, the only dialysis hospital in New York City, if his kidneys stopped processing the fluids.

Thinking of Brady's commentary on energy as a way to read deceit, I thought about the emergency hospital, where there were many vets telling me to keep my expansive optimism, while the look in their eyes betrayed their sentiment that Brady would not make it through the battle he was fighting. They didn't realize—and I couldn't bring myself to tell them—that I had been steadily learning the language of Dog, so I could understand how Brady felt through this process.

I never showed the vets or technicians how tired I was, and I remained cheerful around Brady. When I came home, though, I collapsed into my bed feeling as if I were a wasting carcass. I had begun to lose weight, as Brady was, and my Lyme symptoms were getting loud again. When I was weary, and it was hard to be vigilant over those 70,000 daily thoughts, I wondered obsessively, "Will I lose Brady? Will I lose the love of my life?"

But I kept coming to see Brady, who was perpetually attached to the noisy IV machine, which reminded us in jeremiad tones that medical technology was keeping Brady alive, that he couldn't keep himself alive autonomously with his own immune system at work. It bothered him to have this alien appendage attached to him; he looked somber and his eyes were no longer shining. And I was battle-worn.

One weekend, D flew from Houston to visit Brady and cheer us up. I told Brady Friday evening before I left, "D is coming," and he went berserk and barked at me. I kind of felt like barking and wagging my tail, too. D arrived late that night, and I fell against him. As he hugged me D style by tapping my back, he blurted, "You look exhausted. You're so white. Are you eating enough?" He fluttered around me like his late Russian babushka would have.

Saturday morning, he was raring to visit Brady. D is not fond of hospitals, and I didn't think he was equipped to face the intense atmosphere at the emergency hospital. "Not yet," I cautioned him. "Let's take a short hike in the Ward Pound Ridge Reservation, and let the doctors do their rounds, and then we'll see him."

It was a sunny but crisp day, and the maple trees graced us with an elegant performance of dancing leaves. We disappeared into the woods. We sat on a rock at one point to do an exercise. I had packed two Ball jars, pens, and little pads of paper. I asked D to write everything he was grateful for on separate pieces of paper and put each one in the jar. We then read them out loud to each other, and the positive exercise gradually lifted our spirits. One of D's papers read, "I am grateful for Brady. He has been a great companion to us." It was time to go see our boy.

Brady impishly threw toys on D's lap, and sat up straight with his old boyish attitude, leading D to exclaim: "He doesn't look that bad!" As I was taking our lunch out of the cooler pack, D left the room to go to the bathroom and wash his hands. When he came back, he was shaking.

"I think I'm going to throw up," he said.

"What happened?"

"There was a lady that came in screaming with her limp cat in her arms, 'My cat is dead, please bring him back!' She was so sad!" His eyes grew wet.

"Yeah, that's why I wanted to prepare you this morning for coming here," I said softly.

Brady could tell that he was upset, and he stood up to nudge D's knee and lick his hand. Brady's licks were not a sign of dominance or submission, as an animal behaviorist once suggested. Brady was comforting D, who was supposed to be there comforting Brady. Even at his nadir, Brady remained noble and loving, taking care of his family.

"Let's take Brady for a walk. There's no way that I can eat lunch in this place," D said. I was so accustomed to eating with Brady in the hospital that I had become inured to quotidian crises. The technicians came in the room to undo Brady's port from the IV machine, and wrap his port in a bandage, so that we could go for a walk around the neighborhood.

We were all relieved to have the opportunity to escape and engage in an activity that had been part of our normal daily routine pre-emergency hospital. Brady edged along slowly, and we ambled with him, petting him and praising him for walking so well. There was no one on the neighborhood sidewalks that day, and all of the front lawns seemed deserted, so we had a walk to ourselves. D was still looking pale, and in hopes of boosting our collective morale, I asked, "Remember how happy we were when we became grandparents?" He laughed, Brady glanced up at us with a mischievous look in his eye, and I relaxed at the thought of bringing levity into our day.

When Brady was a little over a year old, we were visiting my grandmother on her farm. It was the ideal spot for a dog, with multiple romping opportunities over a hundred acres. I let Brady out the door early one snowy winter morning to do his morning business. When I looked out the window to check on him, I gasped as I saw another dog's behind stuck to Brady's. "Grandma, there's something wrong with Brady!" She rushed over to look out the window, and started laughing. "They're mating, Michelle, haven't you ever seen that before?" I was horrified and shook my head.

"That's Sadie. She's the Australian shepherd that belongs to Paul." I raced outside in my flannel pajamas to pull the two dogs apart, but that didn't work, so I ran up the hill in the frigid March air towards Paul's house. Paul answered the door as soon as I rapped.

Breathless, I said, "My dog Brady has had sex with your dog Sadie." Paul was tall and middle-aged with a healthy-looking head of brown hair, and he was wearing flannel pajama pants, too. He seemed rather amused by this news.

"Well, there's nothing we can do now. Come in," he gestured. "I'll get you some coffee and pancakes topped with my award-winning maple syrup and we can talk dogs." I looked out his window from the kitchen table and saw that Brady and Sadie had come up to his house, and were engaging in sexual intercourse once again on Paul's lawn. Paul said proudly, "The likelihood of a pregnancy is high." I hid my face in my hands.

About three months later, Paul called and asked if Brady and I could come up and babysit the puppies and Sadie, while he flew out to Seattle for his daughter's graduation. When we arrived, just before we were set to leave for Wisconsin, the dogs seemed to know that Brady belonged to them. Half of them looked like Brady and half of them looked like the Australian shepherd that Sadie was. During the week that I stayed there, the dogs developed an efficient routine, and I was just the spectator that prepared meals.

My Grandmother: Great Grandmother to Brady's and Sadie's puppies.

In the morning, Sadie led the pack of six puppies to the pond below the house, and Brady took up the rear. They all walked in a relatively straight line, and came back in the same rank and file. Then, Sadie, visibly exhausted from breastfeeding, would lie down for her morning meal. Brady would guard her, meaning that he would not let the puppies near her while she was eating. They jumped and climbed on him, which he tolerated without balking, to my astonishment. They all gathered around me after they had finished eating, and we played together, which meant that Brady, Sadie, and I were jungle gyms for the puppies.

Brady chose to sleep with Sadie and the puppies in the kitchen rather than sleep on the bed with me. I felt like a grandmother, and when my own grandmother walked up to the house and cuddled the puppies, I felt like a proud grandmother sharing her grandchildren with their great-great-grandmother. For that one week, I was part of a canine family.

D and I had to come out of our reveries, and walk Brady back to the hospital. D took me out to dinner to boost my spirits. He said, "You know, I'm pretty shaken at how Brady looks. He's wasting away. I don't know how you stand going there every day." When we'd talked on the phone over the previous weeks, he couldn't visualize the descriptions I'd been giving him. And I probably sounded overly confident when I sketched the scene on the phone, assuring D each time that Brady was going to survive this. D ordered a few entrées to go, to reassure himself that I would have enough to eat when he left.

The next morning, D made meals for Brady. Even though I was a raw vegan at the time and could hardly tolerate touching meat, I swallowed my aversion and made cooked meals for Brady. The hospital wouldn't allow us to feed him raw food given the risk of spreading bacteria. D is the king of cooking for his loved ones, though, and so he made batches of chicken, turkey, beef, and salmon for Brady before we returned to the hospital.

D was intent on feeding Brady, so he got on the floor and held out morsels of salmon and chicken. "Good boy, just a little, please?" He kept coaxing Brady with heart-wrenching persistence. Brady turned his head at his favorite treats, and D's shoulders sagged in response. He had to return to Houston that night. "Do you have to go?" I whimpered as the car service pulled into our driveway. "I do. I'm sorry, just please get him to eat. Please," D called out again as he stepped into the waiting car.

We had been brave for D, but Brady and I started showing signs of edginess and breakdown the following week. Brady had been a polite patient when he first arrived, but after some weeks, he was growing weary of the needle pricks. The constant blood tests and catheter changes started to disconcert him, and he began to growl at technicians and lash out at the doctors who were trying to save his life. Brady was frustrated, and the doctors understood this.

I felt so weak one day that a friend insisted on driving me to the emergency room. Uncannily, I ended up on IV fluids myself, with a kidney infection. When I was in the hospital for several hours, all I could think about was visiting Brady. "I don't have time for this," I told the doctor. "I have to be with my dog at the emergency hospital." The doctor shook her head, counseling me: "You can't help him if you can't take care of yourself first. Put your own lifejacket on first!"

While I was in the hospital my friend Jennifer went to visit Brady in my stead. At that point in the afternoon, I hadn't known if they were going to release me that day. Because Jennifer works in the healthcare industry, in close proximity to patients, she had to stay outside of his cage, but she sat and talked to him, like she thought I would have done. They had been friends for a long time.

When I went home from the hospital, I felt like someone had come with a vacuum cleaner and sucked out all of my energy. I called Vijaya, who had been faithfully supporting me. If I was Brady's valiant soldier, she was mine. She drove over to the house that night to guide me through restorative meditations. By morning, I was ready to resume being Brady's strength since he had lost his.

Brady's muscles atrophied alarmingly. His once strong haunches were slight and paper-thin. Watching this gradual atrophy panged my heart. He used to fly over fallen trees like a show horse, race through Mianus River Park in Greenwich, and retrieve sticks until my arms were limp from throwing them. Then, he would enthusiastically swim laps in the watering hole at the turnaround point in Mianus, catching my eye to make sure I was watching him and witnessing his athletic prowess. Now his leg muscles barely supported him.

We started to spend time outside, sitting on a blanket on a strip of green grass behind the emergency hospital. I had pleaded for the privilege. "He needs fresh air. He's spent his whole life in nature." The technicians would drag out his IV stand and hook Brady up to it, while I arranged hospital blankets for us and brought out snacks, treats, and homemade meals for him. He would put his head on my lap and make little sounds of contentment when I stroked his head. He still had flickers of vitality in those soulful eyes.

There was a multi-story office building across from the grassy area, and the employees must have been able to see us from their windows because they would come outside to greet Brady. "Get well, Brady! You can do it!" He thumped his tail at them in feeble acknowledgment. I bundled up in down jackets, scarves, and hats so that Brady would be able to take his fluids outside and have fresh air.

Outdoor IV therapy at VCA emergency hospital.

Even though he was still attached to the IV stand, Brady would lift his face to the sun, close his eyes, and pant with his mouth half open to show his delight at being outside. We were not remotely doing okay, though, if I had been honest with myself at the time. It was becoming increasingly difficult to find a good vein for the catheter, to feed him, to see progress in his acute renal failure case. We were just trying not to go gentle into that good night.

One afternoon, Dr. Whitney came into our room while Brady and I were hanging out. She seemed tense: "Michelle, his creatinine values are going up, and we're concerned about this development. We aren't sure why the aggressive diuresis isn't bringing the creatinine down, so we'll have to increase the volume of fluids per hour." A hurricane system started churning in my chest, but I had a radical idea.

"Could I come back later with a sleeping bag?" I asked hopefully. I must have sounded desperate, because Dr. Whitney nodded. I thought Brady's morale would be boosted if I could stay overnight, perhaps in our room instead of him being in his cage. She did aver that "no one has ever slept over before, but it just might help." I thanked her in my normal adult voice meant for humans, and then I turned to Brady and said in my voice reserved for him, "I'll be back in just a little bit." He cocked his head and panted confidently.

It would be the first night in nearly a month since we had slept in the same room. I hoped that Brady's wolf-like courage would see him through the evening while I made my preparations. The most important item that I put in my overnight bag was Brady's favorite purple bear, his oldest, most treasured possession.

The night receptionists knew to expect me, and by this time, they just shook their heads at the crazy dog lady. "Brady Slater's mom is here to spend the night," they announced over the intercom, gesturing me back towards our room. I didn't consciously think of myself as Brady's "mom," but that's how they saw me, and I didn't want to engage in any philosophical discussions with them about what a human was, or what a nonhuman animal was. This wasn't the time for that.

Brady came through the back door of the room with the tech, elated to see me again so soon, but not surprised because I had prepared him in the language of Dog. I spread out my Marmot sleeping bag that was fit for an expedition, my inflatable mountaineering Thermarest, a few pillows, and extra blankets. Then, triumphantly, I pulled out his purple bear, knowing that it would bring him at least a modicum of pleasure. He pounced on it playfully and fell to the ground holding it between his paws, looking up at me adoringly. His gaze calmed my worried heart.

The year before, I'd been packing for a long trip to Turkey where I would attend a literature conference in Istanbul. Brady knew what it meant each time I brought out the suitcase from the closet and started packing. This time, the packing process took place over an entire week, since I was also packing textbooks and materials for a manuscript that I was writing on 21st century French literature. Just as I was about to drive Brady up to Vermont for the summer, he made a curious gesture. He would make sure that I was watching, and then he would deliberately pick up his favorite toy — the very same well-worn purple bear that he had since he was eight weeks old — and he would carefully place it in my suitcase. Then he would sit back on his haunches and gaze into my eyes directly.

The first few times, I tilted my head at him and smiled, saying "Brady, you aren't going to Turkey with me," and I would take his toy out. Each time, he went back through the steps of putting it back into my suitcase. He knew that he wasn't coming with me. I had told him out loud several times, "Brady is going to Vermont to see Dad and Janet." Brady would stare at me first to make sure he heard me correctly, because he knew this expression, and then, he would prance straight out to sit by the car. Tongue hanging out, confident that he would not miss his ride to Vermont, Brady waited.

"Although I won't be traveling with you to Turkey, I know that you are going to miss me, and I want you to have my favorite toy to think of me while we are separated," he seemed to be saying. The toy went to Turkey with me, and it stayed on my bedside table for the month that I was gone. It was a comfort for me, since I missed him terribly, just as he knew it would be.

The young technician startled me out of my reveries when he came in. "You guys are amazing. I'll be back throughout the night to change Brady's IV bags," he told me cheerfully. They had set up two bags so that one would empty and roll over to a second one, but since Brady was getting one liter per hour, they were quickly changing bags. They would take him out during the night. "We can deal with all of the interruptions, as long as we can be together for one night," I reassured him.

Brady understood that this was a slumber party, and since such events are festive, he wriggled up closely to me, waiting for me to settle into my sleeping bag. He lay down next to me, placed his head on my chest, and heaved a profound sigh. I sighed, too, and we repeated this venting process. I put my arm around him and stroked his back over and over. What decadence to spend the night together. The floor smelled like bleach disinfectant, an IV machine was growling in the background, and it was the most expensive "hotel" we would ever stay in. But we were beside ourselves.

I am very sensitive to noise, and Brady was, too, but we had become accustomed to this noisy IV machine, as his much-needed prosthetic. He would occasionally lift his head to lick my face in appreciation of my company, and I just glowed in his presence, speaking to him in my Brady voice, "You are my biggest love. You are so strong. You are such a warrior. I love you so much." We kept each other's gaze for quite some time, and then we drifted off for the night.

I woke up disoriented and sore, but when I felt Brady's head resting diagonally on my chest and I saw his handsome face watching over me, my entire body melted into the floor. I forgot about my aching body and smiled at him. Brady reached over and licked my cheek when he saw that I had woken up, and he just stared back at me. He thanked me for orchestrating this stolen visit. We stood up gradually to stretch and tried to recreate a longstanding ritual of ours.

In the mornings at home, we made a petting machine. We tried to make a makeshift one at the hospital, but there was an IV machine in our way. Usually, I spread my feet, bend over, and extend my arms straight down in a mechanical petting motion. When Brady saw the petting machine, he came right over playfully, and walked through my arms. I petted him like an automated car wash brushes the sides of a car, moving my outstretched arms back and forth along his sides. He stopped and stretched his hind legs, and then I rubbed his haunches and hind muscles, helping him stretch. He would come through several "washes" in our petting machine. He wagged his tail whenever he saw the petting machine, and he never missed an opportunity to go through it. Even with our awkward petting machine, we were elated in the hospital that morning.

In addition to snuggle and slumber party therapy, I would now be bringing in the most powerful tool I knew: Debbie was coming to Connecticut.

CHAPTER TEN
THE LADY IN THE PURPLE TURBAN TRAVELS TO CONNECTICUT

In mid-October, Debbie was scheduled to fly from North Carolina to lead an animal communication workshop that I had organized to host at my home. When Debbie landed at JFK, she wanted to go straight to the animal hospital to talk to Brady. Although I had never met her in person before, and we had always focused our conversations on Brady, we connected immediately as if we were sisters. We chatted incessantly, oblivious of the Friday afternoon traffic as we inched along to the hospital. After sitting alone with Brady for endless days in the depressing environment of the emergency hospital, I knew that it would be comforting to have Debbie there with me.

Brady greeted her like an old friend, folding his ears back bunny style, nudging her knee with his nose, wagging his tail. Brady reserves such affection for his close friends. This was clearly not an introduction; this was a reunion. Debbie asked for quiet and tuned into him right away. Brady told Debbie that my song about light and home made him stronger. My eyes opened widely in recognition, because every night at the hospital I sang a Snatam Kaur song to him. The refrain was: "May the pure light within you guide your way home." "How many more nights do

I have to spend at the hospital," Brady repeatedly asked. Debbie answered gently, "As many nights as it takes to heal your kidneys." Brady's next question was, "When will I be working with the people?"

When she asked him to explain, he told her that I had already communicated the picture of the workshop to him many times. Debbie asked if he was up for communicating with anyone, and Brady responded that he was very eager to participate. Reluctantly, we left him for the evening.

I had related many of Brady's conversations with Debbie to D, and he usually rolled his eyes, but he was always keen to listen. When I told him that Debbie was coming, he asked, "Will she be wearing a purple turban and long robes?" D happened to be visiting that weekend from Houston, and his astonishment was visible when Debbie arrived wearing jeans and a black turtleneck, sporting a long blond ponytail, looking just like the proverbial girl next door with friendly brown eyes. She has never let D live down the purple turban comment.

On the morning of the workshop, I woke up with great relief that I wasn't in the house alone. D was there, and there was a friend down the hall who could talk to Brady. I made Debbie one of my famous green juices with kale, cucumber, celery, lemon, and ginger to take into her morning meditation.

A family friend, Arthur, was a fellow dog lover, and he had signed up for the workshop as soon as I shared the flyer with him. He drove down from Vermont early to offer his help. This is what Arthur does. Giving gifts, whether they are kind gestures or thoughtful objects, is his love language. Arthur not only has the heart of Santa Claus, but he also looks like him, from his white beard to his rotund tummy and baritone voice. That's how I describe him to everyone. He would later become the fairy godmother to our entire family, from Brady to Dad.

Already Arthur's presence was a boon. After he enveloped me in an avuncular hug, and patted his chest to show his empathy for Brady's plight, Arthur got to work without being asked. It was a crisp October morning, so he set about making a cozy fire, while I arranged coffee and tea on the game table.

There was an air of enthusiasm as people arrived and found their places in the circle. Numerous people had signed up for the workshop. Three I knew, but the rest were people I was meeting for the first time. Debbie welcomed us with one of her warm smiles that I could just feel over the phone every time I talked to her. She settled cross-legged into her striped velvet chair and began speaking about the art of animal communication.

"We are becoming more of a nonverbal species with texting," Debbie said. "Many of us have experienced the uncanny phone call when we were thinking of the caller, or we have experienced an indescribable bond with an animal." Within the first hour, Debbie was guiding us through the preliminary steps and exercises that would help us ground, hone our intuitive skills, and ultimately connect with nonhuman animals. As I observed the participants around me, I could sense their relief as they were able to speak with animals.

As we broke for lunch, Arthur displayed his famous ebullience, as he often did when he was excited, like a "ho ho ho!" "I was worried I wouldn't be able to do this, but I'm really getting these steps! It all makes so much sense." Although Arthur had never heard of Debbie before, many of the participants told Arthur at lunch that they had been waiting years to meet Debbie, and that her method does really work. I couldn't wait for him to hear the animals himself like I had.

I confirmed the irrefutability of animal communication once again when we worked on partner exercises involving one another's animal friends. I paired up with Theresa who wanted me to communicate with her dog Raleigh. Theresa told me that her husband Patrick was skeptical about the notion of animal communication. She wanted to know if Raleigh had any way of making him believe. I had never met Theresa's husband, nor had

I met Raleigh, and I had never been to their apartment. When I found Raleigh on the telepathic airwaves, I made preliminary conversation, and then I asked her if there was any way to make Patrick believe that she could communicate with him. With my eyes closed, I saw a picture in my mind of a bureau in a bedroom. There was a top drawer that had medals in it, underneath some underwear on the right-hand side. Raleigh asked me to tell Theresa about these medals for Patrick's benefit. I heard those words. I thanked Raleigh for communicating with me, as Debbie had taught me to do, and then I returned to Theresa with the revelations.

Theresa stared at me, dumbfounded. "Miche! Those are the medals that Patrick keeps from his deceased relative who was very important to him. I can't believe this!" I told her that this was Raleigh's way of showing Patrick "proof" that she was communicating with me. Theresa was in tears, and she couldn't wait to tell her husband that Raleigh was giving him a sign.

Brady was to have been the model dog that we were to practice on while we learned the rudimentary techniques of animal communication. It was comforting that so many people would be tuning in to speak with Brady while he was alone. Debbie insisted that we tell no one that Brady was in the hospital, so I asked Arthur and Theresa not to mention anything. Debbie circulated a photo of him, along with a list of questions to ask him. She asked us to find quiet places on the property to connect with him in the way that we had been taught. When everyone reconvened in the living room, there were many worried faces. When Debbie asked for feedback, a woman from Cape Cod named Meredith raised her hand and said, "Brady showed me pictures of something that looked like an IV machine; is he okay?" I nearly gasped.

Others quickly echoed Meredith, saying that their body scans revealed a lot of pain, and that he showed them similar pictures inside a building that looked like a hospital. Debbie then revealed that Brady was in the hospital fighting for his life, attached to an IV machine that was supporting his kidneys. One of the participants said, "Brady indicated that he didn't know if he would ever come home from the hospital." My shoulders slumped, but Debbie quickly moved on from this disturbing piece of information, asking what Brady's response was to the question, "What is your relationship with Michelle?" They all provided the answer in unison: "Soul mates!"

I laughed because I have ruminated at length about the nature of my relationship with Brady over the years, and I have settled on the term 'soul mate.' A soul mate, according to Oxford English Dictionary, is a person ideally suited to another; I edit this definition to include all beings, including dogs.

The feeling Brady produced in me, consistently, was what philosopher Hubert Dreyfus described about another philosopher's credo: "The goal of life, for Pascal, is not happiness, or peace, or fulfillment, but *aliveness*."[22] Brady made me feel more alive, and I enhanced his sense of vitality, too. That was my working definition of a soul mate, as someone who brought this sense of aliveness out in me, and vice versa. Brady was definitely my soul mate.

When Debbie and I checked in with Brady later that day, he had a message for all of us: "I feel very honored and special to be receiving so much love and light. Thank you." Debbie said that he connected to everyone yet he felt useless being in the hospital while we were all working on a project that he was meant to be a part of.

On the final day of the workshop, we worked with each other's animals that had already passed away. Arthur broke down sobbing when his communication partner shared what Arthur's childhood dog Sean had to say to him: "I forgive your mother. I have been waiting for this moment to tell you." Later, Arthur told me that his Irish Setter Sean had died under horrible circumstances that were his mother's fault. She had driven over him and dragged him down the driveway. He said that Sean had been his closest friend and confidante, and he didn't think he would ever connect with him again. Arthur felt tremendous relief from the guilt and grief that he had carried for decades. At that moment in the workshop, Arthur knew that "animal communication is real. Time and time again, we acknowledged the factual basis of the animals' comments."

From the look in everyone's eyes, I knew the workshop had been a success, and it lifted me to know that Brady and I had helped create that experience for others.

Chapter Eleven
A Gleeful Kidnapping

On the sunny fall day that Debbie's animal communication workshop concluded, I was feeling buoyed by the positive energy that the workshop participants generated. It made me want to capitalize on that moment. D suggested that I kidnap Brady and take him to the beach, and Arthur and Debbie egged us on. The doctors had disconnected his port so I could take him outside, and I just headed for the door with him and said, "See ya later!" I scooped him in the car—he was far too weak to jump in—and I made for the beach for an unauthorized field trip.

I called D as soon as I had Brady in the car and said, "Meet us at the Norwalk beach." Brady was emaciated; his hind muscles had atrophied to the extent that walking was difficult for him. There were bandages on most of his legs from catheter insertions and he had something like bedsores. His tail was covered in talc powder and wrapped with surgical tape because it had a rash. But he was free, and we were going to profit from every moment in the sea air.

The sun was falling gradually, and we walked slowly along the beach with Brady, who didn't make for the water for the first time in his life. We sat on the sand next to him when he needed to rest. Brady couldn't walk very far, and he stumbled along the way on the sand. He showed me with his soulful eyes just how much he appreciated our outing, and he understood that this was a stolen respite.

I knew it was time to go back because Brady wasn't supposed to be off IV fluids for long. The doctors were only mildly reproachful when we returned. I imagine that they understood, and if Brady had a bucket list, going to the beach would have been on it.

Debbie and Arthur joined us back at the hospital for one more visit, and Brady even wanted to play with Arthur a bit. I was relieved to have friends share our daily burden in these dark times. Brady sat in the center of the room holding court just like old times. In spite of Brady's gaunt appearance, Debbie and I felt optimistic about his strength to recover. Later, though, Arthur confided in me that after he saw Brady's deteriorated condition that weekend at the hospital, he had a "tremendous fear that the veterinarians would call to report that Brady had died while we were having dinner."

It was heart wrenching to return to my daily hospital routine once everyone had left, but Brady seemed a little more energetic in the days following the workshop. Then he plummeted again. I spent more nights at the hospital, but I was getting less and less sleep on the concrete floor. Brady went on a hunger strike to protest the extended hospital stay. When we communicated with Debbie, she said quietly that Brady didn't have as much hope that he would be going home. I began to wonder if I was making a mistake in his care. I think all of us who've had a gravely ill dog have struggled with this: what's right? What's humane?

Was I doing the right thing by Brady by keeping him in the hospital? I asked the doctors if I should just bring him home. "All of the work that we have done so far would be lost," Dr. Whitney said firmly. I didn't get a chance to intervene when my loved ones were sick before, not my mom, and not Joy. This time, for them, for Brady, for myself, I couldn't afford to get this wrong. But was this sterile, stark place of crisis and stress the best place for a free being that had spent his life in a loving home? *Was he going to die in the depressing emergency hospital, and not at least be home in his own bed?* I couldn't let that happen. I owed this to Joy, to Brady, and to Love.

I wasn't going to accumulate any more regrets about Brady. I couldn't bear to after his training trauma at the breeder's. It wasn't until the first conversation that I had with Debbie that I became privy to the painful details of his two-week stay at the breeder. I burst out with the question on the phone: "What happened last summer when he was at the breeder for training?" I didn't give any other details.

Debbie relayed Brady's narrative of abuse to me in fragments. "He felt blindsided when he got there." I waited, my face tingling as it did before a tear storm. "He felt stripped. He didn't know if you were coming back, and he felt like he had done something wrong." Falling tears made rivulets down my cheeks. "He was beaten and yelled at every day, and he didn't know what was expected of him. He felt like he was in prison." Shoulders heaving as the rivulets became torrential, I waited for more.

"There was another dog in a cage right next to him that was very aggressive to him. The other dog was constantly at him, growling at him and he felt like he was going to break. He was insecure when he came home, and he had nightmares. He was fearful of dogs who barked at him. Certain voices remind him of the man who abused him."

"Debbie, can you ask him if he knows that I will never, *ever* put him in a dangerous situation like that again? Please apologize to him, and *please* tell him that I love him." I stuttered as I spoke.

"He knows that he will never go back there again. He knows that you love him more than anyone in the world. He adores you. He says that his purpose is to love you. And to make you laugh. He says that you are very reserved sometimes — he is showing me a picture of a desk where you spend a lot of time — and that he loves it when you leave the desk and play in the water with him." Debbie spoke softly.

When I have been overly involved in my writing, Brady has thrust a toy in my lap as if to remind me to be playful once again — to bring out my endogenous opioids, too. My chest heaved through my tears, and I began to laugh.

"One more thing. He is telling me that your love was a sanctuary for him to heal. He is showing me a picture of the two of you being in a warm den and it is bringing some kind of healing." I didn't entirely understand Brady's imagery, but I distinctly heard the words "healing" and "love." He must have meant the weeks of homegrown PTSD therapy I came up with to comfort him.

Four years later, my love still needed to be a sanctuary for Brady. But this time he was safely in the hospital receiving the treatment that he needed to battle leptospirosis, and I was right by his side, not far away in Turkey. Reflecting on this, I felt a renewed confidence that he *was* right where he needed to be. Even so, I steeled myself to persevere through the battle we were fighting together.

Chapter Twelve
An Unexpected Homecoming

When I left for the hospital in the mornings, the ice on my windshield reminded me just how long it had been since I admitted Brady to the hospital in late summer. Angst and grimness had been easy to dissolve in the beginning. I brought light to my darkest thoughts, and transformed them into hope and perseverance. Yet, after weeks upon weeks without any good news in the doctors' daily updates, I couldn't keep the fear and pain of Brady's demise at bay with my meditation practices. My throbbing joints and Lyme-related chronic fatigue were thwarting my efforts to remain strong for Brady's fight. My body was protesting my sustained role as Brady's soldier. Things were falling apart; the ailing center could not hold much longer.

Dr. Whitney came into our room one afternoon, surprising me. "I'm optimistic for the first time in five weeks because Brady started to self-taper from the fluids, and his creatinine values went down in spite of the taper. His creatinine levels held steady at 1.5 for a few days, and his base fluid rate was reduced by 70 mls." He was still on a high rate of fluids though, between 600 and 700 milliliters an hour, in addition to 170 milliliters per hour base rate. "He will need a slow taper of one week, then he might be able to go home if the taper goes well," she cautiously informed me.

I was starting to dread hospital visits, as Brady was paper-thin and depressed, and I was fighting off tears at the sight of him. Death took place at this facility, and it was starting to get to me. I kept wondering, would it come for us? Are we really only a week away from release?

On a Saturday at the start of November before I went to the hospital, I visited a private estate in Mt. Kisco, New York, that my friend Jérôme had landscaped with thousands of exquisite Japanese maples, fountains, bridges, and Zen walkways. Knowing that I loved Japanese maples, he urged me to visit. It was the quintessential autumnal day, one that would have made me quite happy in the past. Even the maple leaves, worthy of a haiku by Ryōkan, did not console me.

I broke down for the first time while I was walking among the maples. I started sobbing about Brady. I called my close family friend who I call Aunt Beast — in Madeleine L'Engle's *A Wrinkle in Time*, Aunt Beast is the comforting character in the darkest of times — and she decided that she would take a few days off from work, and travel from Vermont to Connecticut the following morning to lend her support.

When I visited Brady that afternoon, he didn't crack a smile; in fact, his somber face and emaciated body mirrored mine. "Rage, rage, against the dying of the light," I wanted to whisper to him. Instead, I held him close and whimpered out loud. Leptospirosis was killing us.

As I was getting out of the car the next day after grocery shopping for Aunt Beast, Dr. Easton, the vet on duty that night, called me: "We're going to release Brady tonight." When I heard the word "release" I sank down onto the pavement in my driveway with my bag of groceries, and I just slouched up against my car. As a few blueberries rolled down the driveway, I thought: *Could it really be? Am I really getting my Brady back? Did Dr. Beth Whitney pull this off?*

I wept tears created by a mixture of exhaustion, ecstasy, and disbelief. My next thought was to call Aunt Beast and tell her that she could turn around and drive back to Vermont because Brady was coming home and we would be fine. Just as I was debating whether to call her, she telephoned to say that she was just an hour away. "I will accompany you to the hospital to bring Brady home, and then we will nurse him together." Nurse him? In my addled mind, if Brady were coming home, it meant that we would return to our old routine and that he would be returned to me as good as new.

I paced around the driveway for a bit in flummoxed disbelief, and then I bustled around the house to make it comfortable for Brady. I brought one of his beds into the kitchen so he could be lying next to us when we were making his home-cooked meals. I brought down all of his water bowls that had been put away in the cupboards, filled them with fresh spring water, and distributed them around the house in their usual spots. I turned up the heat a little, since he had lost weight and might be cold. I fluttered around until Aunt Beast arrived in the driveway.

When I waved at her, she smiled at me through the car window. A wave of relief at not being alone nearly knocked me down. I opened her car door, and she swung her arthritic legs clad in brown wool trousers out to the pavement. She inched up from the seat, vertebrae by vertebrae. Clad in her thick Scottish sweater, knit in alternating stripes of rust, olive, gray, and bark brown — one of my favorites that I may have borrowed once for about a year — she came to a full standing position in my driveway, greeting me at eye level. "Hello, hello there," she said. Her sympathetic eyes beamed at me through her spectacles, and I leaned forward to hug her, careful not to topple her over. Aunt Beast's hug emanated comfort, hence the name.

Aunt Beast and I drove to the hospital to retrieve Brady, chatting about how we would nurse him, and then she stayed in the car to rest while Brady's veterinarians prepared me for the intricacies of his home care. I didn't even get a glimpse of Brady while the doctors were stuffing IV fluid bags into a large box, along with needles and IV lines. Dr. Easton showed me how to tent skin, and insert a syringe, unaware that I was skittish about needles. "You will be giving him two liters a day of subcutaneous fluids," she told me matter-of-factly. I had been hoping to thank Dr. Whitney personally, but she was off-duty that night.

I loaded multiple bags of medical supplies into the car. After this interminable period of learning to become a personal vet tech, they brought out a German shepherd with a handsome face and soulful eyes attached to a paper-doll body of a dog. Brady was barely able to stand up; he weighed about 49 pounds.

I had always kept his red collar in the center console of my car, waiting for the jubilant moment that he would be able to wear it again, like a prisoner released from prison, reunited with his belongings. On what I had imagined would be our victorious moment leaving the emergency hospital after nearly eight weeks, I squatted down, put my left arm under his chest, and with the other I tucked his tail and back legs in, and nestled my arm around his bottom. I bounced right back up with a straight spine and upright head, for I needed to muster enough dignity for two proud individuals.

Brady accepted his ride as if he belonged there in my arms, and this was normative behavior for a regal dog. I opened the back door of my car with my left hand and my knee to settle my darling boy onto the layers of soft, worn quilts I had placed on the backseat of my car just for him. Quilts that I had cuddled with as a child. I shall never forget the look on Brady's face when I turned around to see if he was nestling on the quilts in the back seat. There was a look of quiet joy and a weak smile on his face when he looked directly into my eyes. He knew that he was going home. I had to snap several photographs to document this auspicious moment for us, and the hollow of my chest heaved with quiet joy.

The most hard-fought moment of our life: coming home from the emergency hospital.

Aunt Beast spoke to Brady softly, and he lay his cheek into her hand when she extended it back to him. I murmured to her, hoping Brady wouldn't tune in, "As much as I want Brady to come home, I'm not sure they should have released him. I'm not qualified to administer these medical treatments." She nodded her bobbed gray head in tacit sympathy. I drove home gingerly, avoiding bumps and potholes. We were broken but we were together.

It was dark by the time we arrived home with Brady, and our instructions were to begin the first evening by administering a liter of subcutaneous fluids. I carried Brady into the library where I settled him onto his bed. He sighed faintly and fell into an angelic sleep. He used to fill out his bed, but now he only occupied a corner of it.

Aunt Beast and I were not nurses. I cannot underscore that statement enough. We grossly underestimated the challenge of administering subcutaneous fluids, among many other facets of Brady's MHICU, otherwise known as Makeshift Home Intensive Care Unit. It took Aunt Beast and I two and a half hours to conduct this procedure that the vets said would take 20 minutes.

We had to figure out how to attach the needle to the line, the line to the bag of saline fluids, uncap the needle, squeeze the bag until the air bubbles came out of the needle, and recap the needle. Then, I had to tent Brady's skin by pulling it up taut and sticking him with the gigantic needle hole-side up. Aunt Beast unclamped the fluids, and then she squeezed the bag as hard as she could until Brady had a massive hump on his back, and the bag was crumpled and dry. Brady slept through the entire procedure, thankfully.

We were both spent. Aunt Beast's arthritic hands throbbed from squeezing so hard. I was traumatized by thrusting an 18-gauge syringe in the back of my loved one, particularly since I had never wielded a needle before unless I was sewing. And to think that I had nearly sent Aunt Beast home before Brady was discharged. We stared at one another in wonder. Then Aunt Beast asked the dreaded question: "How will we repeat this process in the morning?"

Aunt Beast was an even more unlikely candidate for Dog Nurse than I was, because she was a devout Christian Scientist. That means that she has eschewed all medical procedures and medications in favor of prayer treatment.

It's a testament to her love for us that she participated in these medical acts that contradicted her staunch principles. Knowing this, I was even more awed by her help.

I had to carry Brady up the stairs to my bedroom because he couldn't even walk over a doorsill without tripping and falling. He was so meek when I picked him up and so weightless that I could carry him up two flights of stairs effortlessly. I walked down the hall to my bedroom and made a beeline for the bed.

When I placed him on my down duvet up by the pillows, he heaved a sweet sigh that reverberated through me. He was palpably relieved to be at home in his own bed. I just stood there, stared at him, breathed deeply, and exhaled my own sigh. "This is a miracle, my love," I whispered.

We're home and Brady is alive, I kept repeating as if to convince myself as I brushed my teeth. He would not be sleeping on a desolate concrete floor that night. He didn't have perfect kidneys, but we had exceeded the expectations of the kidney specialists. I discovered supportive text messages from D and Janet as I was going to bed, "Good job, you really saved him. You did it." D wrote. "Dad and I are elated that Brady is home," Janet added.

Before we left the hospital, Brady sent me the distinct message that he merely wanted to breathe me in. "I just want to bask in you. Just lie down and feel my heartbeat," he requested. When I went to bed, we lay entwined on my bed so that he was lying across the pillow with his head on my chest. We made half of a capital T. I think that he was asking that after the aberration of the hospital routine, could we engage in the ordinariness of merely existing together?

Brady is relieved to be on his own bed after having spent two months in the emergency hospital.

When I snuggled up with Brady that night, neither of us moved from our nesting places all night long, and we slept profoundly. I woke up feeling like it was Christmas when I realized that Brady was curled up on my shoulder instead of being alone in a hospital cage. There was no early morning phone call to make, no kidney values to write down on my bedside notepad. I wept while Brady licked the tears before they could fall.

After a harried breakfast, I called Dr. Mike. "Brady is home! We need help." Smith Ridge Vet gave us the green light to come at once. We picked Brady up and put him in the car, and drove off through the woods for just a few miles to Dr. Mike's.

At the renowned holistic hospital that Dr. Marty Goldstein founded, veterinarians believe that sickness is an excuse to get healthy, and that the body has the extraordinary ability to heal if we give it the opportunity. I had always agreed with him and his team wholeheartedly. In their parking lot, I have seen license plates from Nevada, Ohio, North Dakota, and many other states. I felt lucky that they were in my backyard.

I'll never forget when I brought Brady in for his first appointment when he was eight weeks old. I trotted in proudly, knowing that the handsome puppy by my side was sure to make fast friends. Rachelle at the front desk called out, "I've been waiting to see him!" We felt very special there, and we were known. They knew that Brady was my soulmate dog.

When I opened the door and carried Brady in, all of his friends from the past six years gathered around him. Dr. Mike opened the door to his office and got right down on the floor to open his arms. "Come here, you big boy."

Dr. Mike was Brady's head doctor once again. Sporting sneakers and Brooklyn hipster spectacles that framed his kind brown eyes, he loved my boy. Brady licked Dr. Mike's face and thick brown beard weakly with his ears folded back bunny style.

Dr. Mike examined Brady thoroughly, and decided that we would be coming for a check-up everyday until we could strengthen Brady. "He's out of the acute renal failure phase, and now we have a chronic condition to tend," he explained. "Could we have some tips on subcutaneous fluid administration?" Aunt Beast asked, hopeful.

When he left the room for a moment to get a colleague, Aunt Beast exclaimed, "He's wonderful! What a different environment from the emergency hospital. They are so loving here, and it's calm and peaceful." I laughed.

"Indeed. And there's no scent of bleach."

"We were tenting Brady's skin too far down his back. Now we can do it closer to his neck." A.B. said.

I nodded.

"Wait? Who is this we? You mean me! I have to insert a gargantuan needle into the neck of the one I love most in this world." We laughed.

Dr. Mike realized that A.B. and I were completely overwhelmed by the subcutaneous fluid project, so he saw to it that we had help. We would come twice a day, and the technicians would administer Brady's fluids. We practically panted in relief.

His colleague Dr. Ruskin brought her worn meditation cushion into the room, and sat on the floor in front of Brady. She looked like a keeper of ancient knowledge. She began our Qi Gong treatment. I use the determiner "our" because Dr. Ruskin's treatments benefited both Brady and me; even Aunt Beast felt the energetic effects. Animals and their humans are receptive to Qi Gong treatments because of the strong energetic connection between them.

Qi Gong is a healing modality that originated in China approximately 4,000 years ago. It's the science and art of using breath, movement, and meditation to circulate life force energy, or Qi, as it's called in Chinese medicine. Qi Gong means *to nurture life*.

Dr. Ruskin closed her eyes and started moving her arms in rhythmic patterns that made me feel peaceful, too. She opened her eyes 20 minutes later to convey that as she was tuning into Brady's meridian energies—or energetic pathways through the body—she perceived that he had a headache, hunger, and that yams would be beneficial to him. She explained that she had been aligning his meridian energies. I agreed with the clinic's philosophy of using an array of tools to keep animals healthy, even if I couldn't chart whether they were effective.

Dr. Mike then gave Brady an acupuncture treatment, along with some homeopathic remedies. I believe in the potential of these tools, but although I refused to consider it at the time, it was obvious that there was no guarantee of success. Even as I looked at him under the lights of Dr. Mike's examination room, I could count each individual rib on Brady.

I didn't want people to see Brady and think he was dying. When we lived in Wisconsin, I purchased a red fleece coat that said DOG in capital letters; it was the last large dog coat in stock. I thought the DOG label was absurd, and thought of finding a matching red coat that read HUMAN. Since it was frequently below zero in Wisconsin when we walked in the mornings, though, the fleece coat had been a necessity. When we got home from the vet, I put it over his shivering body, and attached the fleece straps under his belly with the Velcro tabs. He relaxed into it, grateful for the extra warmth. Seeing him in the red baggy coat helped divert my anxious thoughts from seeing his thin frame. Although I had raised the heat in the house, we had to put a flannel-covered heating pad on Brady's back under his fleece coat to keep him from shivering. Brady reached up to nuzzle my hand and rest it there.

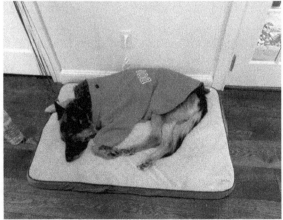

Brady fighting for his life.

My friend Jennifer who had visited Brady when he was in the hospital came over the day he returned home; she brought balloons and treats for him. He couldn't move from his bed, but she sat with him and petted him. Jennifer is a spiritually strong person, and she was the only friend I would let visit Brady during these critical first few days. I feared that others would be frightened by his appearance, but she just enveloped him in her love and gave him her moral support.

Aunt Beast and I devoted ourselves to Brady's care. It took nearly all day to ferry him to and from Dr. Mike's office for twice-daily visits. We went through an elaborate process to cook homemade meals for Brady. His kidneys would no longer process the raw diet he had subsisted on for nearly six years. Raw meat was too rich in protein, and therefore unfriendly to his kidneys. We cooked organic yams, turkey, and free-range, antibiotic-free, hormone-free chicken. We spoon fed Brady since he was almost too weak to stand up from his bed and eat. Dr. Mike said to feed Brady every three hours, and we were making each meal fresh.

My once immaculate kitchen resembled a disaster zone. It looked like a cross between a nursing station — with multiple medications and explanatory sticky notes spread out across the counter — and an amateur kitchen with very messy cooks who used every spare pot and dish in the house. I couldn't believe that Aunt Beast had miraculously descended on us from Vermont at the most needed time. I would have staggered under these tasks if alone.

But we were nowhere near out of the woods. Brady knew it when he gave us grave glances, and we knew it when he slept all day under his heating pad, wrapped in a fleece blanket, in a very warm house.

Following Brady's discharge from the hospital, we communicated at frequent intervals through Debbie. Although I could communicate with Brady, it felt laborious to tune in, whereas Debbie and Brady spoke seamlessly on the telepathic level. Debbie tuned into Brady's high-level thoughts. I currently speak the language of Dog on the intermediate level, yet Debbie speaks so fluently that she instructs Dog. I could never have transcribed the following communiqué.

Centuries after Montaigne stated that our dogs speak to us, late French philosopher Jacques Derrida rephrased the question whether the animal speaks. "Does it speak?"[23] The answer is yes, although we'll unpack that later. I turn once again to the voice of Brady, as translated by Debbie. When Brady had the opportunity to speak, he was garrulous:

I hated being in the hospital because of the heavy energy, and because I felt useless. In the hospital there were a lot of negative comments, fear, no light, and weeds. There was a never-ending staircase and I felt discouraged because I couldn't see the top and it was hard to muster the strength to continue. I could not have done it without her. She [Michelle] kept telling me "just a few more steps." She gave me the hope that eventually I could stop climbing that staircase and reach the light. She was my lifeline, and she kept cutting down the weeds around me so I could follow the light. She saved me. I learned the spiritual lesson that anything is possible, but that I shouldn't be discouraged when it doesn't happen quickly. Her love and confidence kept me going and my love for her made me strong; I trusted her.

When it came to speaking about his experience in the emergency hospital, Brady was reluctant to return to that dark period of our lives, but I asked what he learned from the experience in the hospital.

"I learned to trust and wait," Brady said.

Debbie reiterated that the visual image Brady was showing her was that I was his lifeline through this. He showed Debbie a picture of himself drowning, with me holding out a rope for him.

As frayed as the lifeline had become, I knew that Brady still needed it, and I kept extending it. An emerging problem was that I was beginning to need a lifeline, too.

115

CHAPTER THIRTEEN
TEAM BRADY TO THE RESCUE

It was becoming increasingly difficult to take care of Brady in Connecticut because he couldn't navigate the steps. There were steps going from room to room in my 1930s house, which had been constructed long before the American Disabilities Act passed and architects started taking the notion of accessibility seriously. Even on the main floor, there were steps going from the foyer to the dining room, and from the foyer to the living room. Even the tiny two-inch threshold on the dining room entryway would cause Brady to trip and fall, with his legs splayed out helplessly beneath him. Brady couldn't walk on the slippery hardwood floors either, so I spread out yoga mats in the kitchen as a path between his bed and his food and water bowls. We clearly had a disabled dog on our hands.

I was still carrying him upstairs every night—fueled by adrenalin, because it caused me pain—fretting that I was hurting him, or that it would make him feel helpless, and I consulted with Debbie about this. "He tries to be still when you carry him. He says that you taught him how to handle getting help graciously. That's his way of surrendering." I had been meditating incessantly to surrender; now, Brady was surrendering, too.

In spite of the meditations, and the full-time nursing, we were in disarray.

I had depleted all of my reserves and even the hidden reservoirs beneath those reserves. As much as I meditated and released my stress, I had devoted over two months to saving Brady, and the toll on me was quite significant. I was gaunt, too, albeit not as emaciated as Brady was. I can be a titan when I'm focused on an important task — whether it's running a marathon, getting a Ph.D., or nursing a dog back to health — to the extent that I become oblivious of the toll the grueling task takes on me. But the titan in me was under siege this time, beaten down by spirochetes that I couldn't just ignore in order to press on.

Aunt Beast suggested that she care for Brady while D and I went on a vacation that we had planned nearly a year beforehand, and that was non-refundable. I was very reluctant to go, but Aunt Beast assured me that this was the best plan, and that I would regain my strength while she cared for Brady along with Dad and Janet. We decided to move Brady from Connecticut to a house in Vermont that had been designed for my disabled dad; it would be far more suitable.

Before I consented to this, I knew that we would need to find a miracle doctor in Vermont. Sonja, our family florist in Montpelier, had frequently mentioned that a Cornell-trained vet had saved her cherished dog Baxter. "Dr. Nate Heilman is the most compassionate vet," Sonja gushed. When she told me that his philosophy marries Western allopathic medicine with Chinese veterinary herbal medicine, I was convinced.

She put me in touch with Qi Vet, his holistic clinic in Shelburne, an hour from Dad's house. Without meeting Dr. Nate in advance, I placed all of my trust in him.

When I recount this bizarre narrative, I realize that I was operating outside of my faculty of reason to leave Brady and travel to another continent when we had just been reunited, and he was fighting even harder for his life. Especially when Guilt and Grief long knew how to torment me. Asking for help had always been anathema to my principle of self-reliance, too, but I would have to ask

117

for more help than ever before to pull this next feat off in the name of saving Brady.

Aunt Beast couldn't drive Brady to Vermont by herself, for she wouldn't be able to pick Brady up out of the car or hold the leash while he relieved himself. I felt awkward asking Arthur to fly from Vermont to New York, but he happily agreed to be part of Team Get Brady to Vermont. Arthur arrived early one November morning at JFK. After one last bag of fluids at Dr. Mike's, and one last round of Reiki and Qi Gong from Dr. Ruskin, the motley trio set off for Vermont. I had given Aunt Beast my credit card to use for Brady's expenses. I entreated her to stop at Aux Délices in Westport, to load up with gourmet goodies for the drive, as a paltry way to show my gratitude for their grand gesture.

At the airport, I received a jubilant text message from Aunt Beast. "Brady hopped into the front seat while we were at Aux Délices!" After sending off that ecstatic text, Aunt Beast passed out for the remainder of the drive. She had been head nurse for a dog that should have still been in an intensive care unit, after all. Arthur, on the other hand, was thinking more lugubrious thoughts, as I found out much later: *What if Brady dies on the way to Vermont?*

Team Brady in Vermont consisted of my doting father, my good-natured stepmother Janet, Aunt Beast, and Arthur, who lives a mile from the house. With the exception of Aunt Beast, who still worked for an accounting firm, Team Brady was retired. Dad's house was well outfitted to be a makeshift home intensive canine rehabilitation unit. Since Dad was in an electric wheelchair, he built a one-story house with no steps to negotiate. Between the radiant heat in the floors and the consistent 80-degree temperature—intended to keep my father warm since he had circulation issues—Brady would have the warmth that his fragile body needed.

Dad's unwavering belief in Brady's recovery was his major contribution. "I wasn't afraid when I saw how emaciated he was," he explained later. "I had every expectation that he would gain weight. I was grateful that everyone was pitching in to do everything that they could to help Brady. He was certainly doing his part. He was very receptive to everyone's help, and he was very patient," he later said. Perhaps my optimism was genetically inherited.

Arthur is petrified of needles. Their mere presence causes him to feel faint. Without being privy to this fear at the time, I asked Arthur if he would insert needles in Brady twice daily for the duration of my seven-day absence. Arthur didn't want to disappoint me, and he knew that no one else could do it. *Aunt Beast and Janet surely wouldn't have the fortitude to face that task,* he thought. Arthur told me that the process of preparing Brady for fluids was an intricate production that they took very seriously.

I had given Aunt Beast my iPod to use while Team Brady was administering fluids, and she played Krishna Das to calm Brady. I found out later that Arthur and Janet were not fond of Krishna Das. "The music was horrible," Arthur said. "I absolutely could not listen to that voice drumming away endlessly about Baba Hanuman." Arthur was trying to concentrate on sending positive thoughts to Brady, and he was bristling against this "amorphous genre of noise." A professional vocalist who preferred the Baroque period, Arthur hated to admit that the music had a visible calming and comforting effect on Brady.

Janet was struggling with the chanting, too. With her dry Maine sense of humor, she would whisper to Arthur after a third of the bag had been administered, "Arthur, would you like to dance with me to Krishna Das after we finish the fluids?" "I would heave a bit, but refrain from laughing, so Aunt Beast would offer me another pillow because she thought I was having a muscle spasm," Arthur said. It sounded hilarious, if only Brady had not been dying.

"Michelle, you cannot imagine how it was for us."

"Oh?" I said, "Please enlighten me."

"Your dad kept saying reassuring things to Brady. I would get exhausted from the Reiki and the fluids. It was hard to keep Brady still for 45 minutes. So, I would prick him, then sometimes the needle would come out and I would need to prick him again, then the fluids would fly over the floor, and then I would take the bag and squeeze it. Janet and Aunt Beast had a hard time squeezing the bag, so I would do the needle while Janet was holding the bag, and then I would take over squeezing the bag. We would say, 'Don't move, Brady,' and he would understand and stay! There was an enormous fear involved because we all knew how much you loved Brady. We are responsible people, but this is your baby, and it was such a gift that you trusted us. That was the subconscious thought, and we would compliment each other that you trusted us."

I had put all of my trust in Team Brady, asking them to continue the work of saving my soulmate dog. Was I asking for an impossibility? Did I burden them too much?

Thinking back, I know that I was insane to have left Brady. Depleted as I was, it was surreal to be in Japan when Brady was still fighting for his life. D and I called home every day, and we wrote healing messages at Shinto prayer shrines for Brady, like this: "We wish beloved Brady a full recovery. May he be stronger and healthier than before and may he live to be a wise old German shepherd, surrounded by his loving family and nature." We walked around the hallowed temples of Kyoto in a quasi-stupor, though.

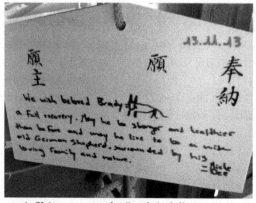

A Shinto prayer for Brady's full recovery

Visiting Japan had long been our dream, and I was an adherent of the Japanese aesthetic of wabi-sabi. The idea of seeking beauty in the imperfections of things appealed to me as the ultimate aesthetic principle. In wabi-sabi, the most sublime object was the one with a hairline crack in it, reminding the spectator of the intransience of this world. We came across examples of wabi-sabi throughout Japan, but instead of fully appreciating them, I wondered why I was strolling among elegant Japanese maples and temples, and sitting in healing Japanese hot springs in the mountains while our precious boy was still so fragile.

Meanwhile, Team Brady was working around the clock. Aunt Beast moved temporarily into my parents' home, and she dubbed herself Head Nurse. HN saw that Brady received all 19 medications, Chinese herbs, supplements, and homeopathic remedies throughout the day, and she oversaw his visits to Qi Vet. Dr. Nate insisted that Brady eat small meals every four hours, which consisted of puréed organic yams, ground pork, turkey, puréed kale, broccoli, and celery. Head Nurse was cooking and feeding home-cooked meals throughout the day for Brady. Have I told you that Aunt Beast is also a vegetarian?

Janet dreaded taking Brady's red fleece DOG coat off to wash it before his first meeting with Dr. Nate, because it hid his stark ribs. She wouldn't let anyone take him out until she had finished washing and drying it; meanwhile, he lay in front of the fireplace shivering. The duties were coming to an end since I would be returning the next day from Japan.

As soon as we landed at JFK, I powered on my iPhone. Twelve hours is a lengthy measure of time to be offline when one is remotely overseeing a loved one's care. I listened to my father's succinct message first. "Ah, please call me posthaste. There has been an unfortunate incident."

My mind flew to Brady and I called at once. "Dad, what is going on?" I shouted as the plane bumbled down the runway. "Michelley! Everything is fine, but there was a... a... " My father did not frequently stumble on his words. "There was a bite."

My face contorted into a grimace, and I asked, "Who did he bite?"

Dad paused. "Arthur."

The magnitude of that revelation devastated me. Arthur had gone to extreme lengths to care for him. How could Brady have bitten him? I was in tears as we exited the plane, and I was determined to drive to Vermont immediately. I called Arthur as soon as we cleared passport control.

"Michelle, I'm... I'm fine! It wasn't about me at all. Brady reacted in pain. He didn't even see me. It was instinctual. He cried out because we pricked him in a place that was raw from so many needle pricks. We were so confident and felt successful that we had made it to this point. We just weren't mindful and we rushed in." Arthur explained that he had always approached Brady from the side, but that last time he came in head on. "I didn't take the time to reassure him and connect with him. However, as soon as I pricked him, he lashed out and started biting me in my stomach, about three times. Janet was hysterical and I was bleeding profusely."

I was biting my lips and my inner cheeks as I listened. Although I understood that Brady had been tested beyond the limit of what any being could endure, I had entrusted him to the care of my other loved ones, and I expected Brady to treat them respectfully. I was berating myself for having left Brady. *How irresponsible of me,* I thought. Arthur continued, at my prodding, with a long monologue.

"I can't explain this, but I was so connected with him that I could just hear him saying, 'I'm done with this.' I felt bad about the whole thing, and that I had hurt him, and I was holding back tears, and the thought of hurting him was horrible, so I just let him bite me. I was just thinking, 'I don't know your pain, but you poor guy.' It hurt badly when he bit me, but I transcended the flight-or-fight instinct. Right after he did it, I took him out for a walk. I didn't take it personally, Michelle. If I hadn't gone through the telepathy workshop, then I wouldn't have understood, but Brady and I were completely at peace with one another afterwards. Brady licked my face to apologize. I understood that he was doing that."

I wasn't satisfied at all. "I'm so sorry, Arthur," I kept repeating, numbly and inadequately. Later, I asked Arthur, "Do you resent me for having left him with you?"

"No," Arthur said emphatically. "Not ever once. I had seen you on that cold, miserable hospital floor with him ten hours a day. It was so important to us for you to get a respite. We all agreed that it was urgent for you to get rest."

I did need proper rest after the past two months. Although it felt wrong to be in Japan, the trip did rejuvenate me. I had regained my serenity and strength; I was ready to resume nursing Brady back to his shining self.

Arthur had one more important thing to tell me. "Brady was seamless in transferring his trust in you to us." I understood that Brady had made a tacit agreement with Team Brady. I don't think anyone could give Brady enough credit for trusting everyone through this experience. His limits were tested, too. Like Arthur, Dad, Janet, and Aunt Beast, I, too forgave Brady. When I consulted with Debbie, she said, "Brady didn't even know that Arthur was there. It was a purely instinctual reaction to pain. He feels quite badly."

Ludwig Wittgenstein, the recondite philosopher of ordinary language and skepticism, writes in *Philosophical Investigations* that we cannot *know* the pain of the other, since we cannot feel it ourselves, but we can *acknowledge* the pain of the other, as a way of accepting that another being exists.[24] Arthur was *acknowledging* the pain that Brady — the other — felt, and in doing so, he was accepting his identity as a fellow being, which, as I listened to Arthur, was a critical point for me. Wittgenstein wouldn't have included nonhuman animals in his discussions on pain, but I'm taking certain liberties here, which I'll come to later.

When I pulled into my dad's driveway, and Janet opened the door with her customary charming welcome, I hugged her tightly as Dad called out an effusive greeting. Over her shoulder, I saw Brady. I went into an ecstatic trance dance.

This reunion eclipsed all of the previous spectacular ones. Brady danced around me whimpering and wagging in joy before he could even calm himself enough to greet me. When he did, I bent down and matched the love in his eyes with my own. He licked every square centimeter of my face until it was dripping in saliva. Finally, he sat and leaned against me, panting contentedly. My chest hummed with the joy that only Brady could bring me. That intertwined DNA we shared was no longer stretched across oceans.

In spite of the nursing around the clock, Brady was still in dire need of ongoing medical attention. I took note of his ability to dance around me when I arrived in Vermont, but he was soon back on his bed fast asleep. His weight was not going up quickly enough, and his red blood cell count—or hematocrit—was not increasing according to Dr. Nate's plan. I was about to meet this Dr. Nate who was working overtime to save Brady's life.

CHAPTER FOURTEEN

DR. NATE HEILMAN, A 21ST-CENTURY ST. FRANCIS

Dr. Nate Heilman had been nursing Brady through tenuous times when the blood panels hinted at narratives of demise, but this time he would be doing it with Brady's fiercest advocate by his side. When we arrived at Dr. Nate's clinic that morning, Jess, his office manager, said, "Brady is a very special guy here." Exuding calmness, Dr. Nate came walking down the hallway with his hand outreached to meet me. He was smiling and he had wise eyes. I imagine that he was about my age, in his late 30s, but I couldn't be sure. He was dressed in what I call Vermont athletic attire, something like a mixture of Patagonia fleece and L.L. Bean. Dr. Nate was the recipient of much tail thumping, folding back of the ears, and hand licking. "What you're doing with him is nothing short of remarkable. It's an honor to take care of him," Dr. Nate told me in a sincere tone.

We went into a consultation room, and Dr. Nate wrote on the whiteboard as he explained medical terms and results that he would like to see. "It's critical that we raise Brady's red blood cell count to increase the oxygen circulation to his body's tissues." He spoke in a professorial tone. I nodded my head, having heard this from Dr. Mike. "He needs a higher red blood cell count to increase his chances of vitality, simply put," he said.

"I'm devoted to saving Brady's life," I promised. "I can't thank you profusely enough."

"It's apparent that you are," he said. We took each other very seriously, and we were on a mission.

Three days a week, I rose early in the morning to drive Brady to Shelburne, Vermont, so that he could spend approximately ten hours on IV fluids receiving treatments from Dr. Nate and his staff. During the day, I explored Burlington, and its quirky, eccentric character was just right for me. I strolled by street musicians and leftie orators on Church Street, designated for pedestrians only, on my way to the coffee shop where I spent much of my day.

People are friendly in Vermont, and they invariably asked me why I was visiting Burlington. As soon as I mentioned that my dog was under the aegis of Dr. Nate Heilman, locals smiled and nodded their heads knowingly in admiration. One story encapsulates Dr. Nate's singular ethos, and I will relate it as the local bookseller at Phoenix Books told it to me.

One winter, there was a woman in Burlington who lived in a broken-down car with her three dogs. She'd lost her home. One of her dogs was ill during the winter, and several vets refused to treat the dog. Someone recommended that she take her dog to Dr. Nate Heilman at Qi Vet. The woman appeared at Dr. Nate's on a cold Vermont day with her three dogs. When Dr. Nate saw her, not only did he treat her dog and nurse it back to life, but he also sheltered the woman and her three dogs at his home all winter. He and his wife nursed them back to health, and sheltered them from the harsh Vermont winter. As I listened to the bookseller's story, I thought how much like a contemporary St. Francis he seemed.

When I asked Debbie how Brady would characterize Dr. Nate, Brady said, "Dr. Nate has white light coming out of his fingers." Debbie said she had never heard anything like that before in all her years of communicating with animals. Brady's extrasensory perception confirmed for me that Dr. Nate was a true healer.

When I picked Brady up, I would sit quietly on the bench in the foyer, but Brady would always start to howl at that moment. The girls would tell me with amazement that he had been resting quietly all day. "He telepathically knows I'm here," I said, without any further explanation. As soon as I heard frantic paws on the floor, I knew he was careening down the hallway to get to me. We reunited every single evening with prancing, licking, and exclamations of joy. Please don't accuse me of having a deep-seated impulse to anthropomorphize at this point.

Brady had lost so much muscle mass that Dr. Nate had suggested a canine massage therapist for him. Canine massage increases joint flexibility, and alleviates muscle and joint pain; it can even benefit the immune system. Sherry would travel to Dad's house from northern Vermont, nearly two hours away. She massaged Brady's enervated muscles, and she taught me how to massage his hind quarters to promote muscle growth. When I spoke with Brady through Debbie, I wanted to know if I was doing a good job massaging Brady. "Meaty section is good, take thumb and forefinger, and just trace a line down back portion, right hind, hock, and trace all the way down. Alternate." Brady was sending me a picture of what I needed to do, and I was seeing it as he was sending it to Debbie.

Everyone who subscribed to the philosophy that it takes a village to save a dog celebrated Brady's birthday on December 7th, 2013. I didn't care if it was a bit kitschy or over the top. I ordered cakes from New England Culinary Institute's La Brioche bakery in Montpelier that read "Happy Birthday Dear Brady." I decorated the house with helium birthday balloons and Sonja made exceptional arrangements at her Botanica floral shop with roses and wildflowers in honor of Brady's recovery, a process she had been tracking closely. I procured birthday gifts for Brady from Quirky Pet in Montpelier, and for Team Brady, too. I ordered a platter of sandwiches and gourmet foods, and made a special "Brady's Birthday Party 2013 Playlist," full of celebratory songs. I invited Aunt Beast, Arthur and his family, and Brady's 'godfather' Jim. Dad and Janet were delighted to host the party, and Brady knew that something special was in the air for him, because he kept giving me contented looks that I thought said, "I know you are doing something special for me. I accept, and I am very pleased. What an honor."

When the appointed day came, I woke up with excitement. Brady had lived and triumphed to his sixth birthday. He was filling out and he looked relaxed. "Happy birthday. Have I told you today how much I love you?" I asked him. He walked around me in circles and I petted him on his head and neck. I sat down on the floor and he licked my face and let me hug him. Then he sat between my stretched-out legs for a minute and let me give him a massage and whisper things like, "You are the love of all of the loves," and "You are so brave." Then he nudged my wrist; it was time for a birthday walk.

Brady bounded through the snow, and I watched how agile he was with quiet joy. It was not a long walk, but it was imbued with the sheer triumph of survival. I put a bandana around his neck that had motley balloons on it with the words "Happy Birthday." He knew that this was his day, and that he could be exactly where he thrived: the epicenter of everyone's focus. Brady greeted each of his friends at the door with much circling and wagging of the tail. We all wore cone-shaped birthday party hats, and everyone took turns petting Brady and posing for photographs with him.

Brady's birthday party photographs ratify my decision to support his healing journey through leptospirosis, and they tell a story. As I scroll through the photos, I pause and rest on an image of Aunt Beast in a rose sweater leaning down to put her arms around Brady's side. Brady is sitting upright with his grand lion-colored forearms spread out before him, his head held high with pride. Brady knew that Aunt Beast devoted herself to him; he knew that he had rallied beautifully for his loved ones, and he knew that he was being celebrated. The photo radiates this extraordinary mélange of love, pride, gratitude, confidence, and celebration. Subsequent photos show Aunt Beast gazing into the camera, revealing her pride and delight in having saved Brady. These photos are gifts and rewards after a battle to rage against the dying of the light. Our light did not die, and we have the photos to prove it.

A jubilant birthday party with Aunt Beast, head nurse.

Brady's eyes met with each pair of ours, and he lay in the center of our circle, basking in the well-merited birthday attention. He nosed his way into multiple birthday bags, and gently pulled out fleece bears, fleece geese, jolly balls, a new fleece coat, and a reflector coat for evening walks in the winter when light would be scarce.

On behalf of Brady, I handed out birthday bags to Aunt Beast, Janet, and Arthur with T-shirts that read, "I kissed a dog and I liked it," and "Life is better with a dog." Everyone was thrilled, and played along with my silliness.

Arthur's son Zach is a professional photographer (who inherited his father's kindness, though not his Santa-like appearance), and he snapped a photo of me and Brady that afternoon that I shall always cherish. After partying, I was ready for a short dognap myself. As everyone conversed around us, I lay down next to Brady. In the photograph, Brady is lying on his stomach with his head up, looking dignified. I am lying on my back at a slight angle away from his body, with my knees bent and my feet on the ground. My head is resting right between his paws. My face is turned towards his face, just inches away from his relaxed tongue, which is hanging out the side of his mouth. My eyes are closed, and I look peaceful. My long blond hair is strewn across Brady's paws and tangled in it. Brady's contented look says, "I am with my girl and all is right in the world."

Napping with my Soul Mate Dog on his 6th birthday upon his release from the hospital. Photo credit: Zach Zorn

I marveled at the extraordinary kindness of Team Brady, and at the community we had created around Brady's care. When I was a girl, my mother and Joy had died so swiftly, and I had no power to intervene. I had felt so lonely as I grieved their inexplicable losses, and I tried to be a superstar so I wouldn't give Dad any further burden. Yet now, somehow, I had been able to intervene and play a major role in the recovery of my loved one. I had agency.

Not only that, I had a community of loving people that also believed in us. This was a gift that Brady brought to me: people showed me their love for me by taking care of him. Brady was the conduit for radiating this pure love. It was another way that we spoke to each other in the language of Dog by giving love and care for each other, like Tah-Kloma and Náhani. And we had a pack that had our backs. They had a heightened awareness of our needs because of all we'd been through, and we had a profound appreciation that we had their extraordinary support.

This was a monumental shift from my girlhood solitary grief and helplessness to a community of supportive love. Brady ushered in a transformation in Dad, too. He'd been just as powerless as I was when Mom and Joy died, and he hadn't been able to acknowledge the pain of his grief at that time. Now, Dad was able to show his love and compassion for me and for Brady in our darkest hours of need. Dad gave his love to Brady and to me as his great contribution to Brady's healing. Dad's ability to remain present for me as I shared my fears about Brady, and Dad's outpouring of love for Brady healed him, too. This time, we both had agency and presence. Brady's illness helped heal me and Dad; Brady showed us what it's like to be enveloped in a loving community rather than suffer a great tragedy alone, like we did when we were younger. That was Brady's gift to us in the midst of his illness.

◦〰◦

We continued our treatment plan with Dr. Nate through December. He was pleased to see both Brady's weight and hematocrit increase, while his kidney values stayed down where we wanted them to be. Brady was a very good sport about all of this, and he even played along with the meal plan. By early January, I was still in Vermont, picking up Brady from Dr. Nate when he said, "Brady is out of the woods. We made it." It was so casual, so calm, so beyond my comprehension. "Out of them?" I articulated each word separately. He nodded with joy in his eyes. "You two are amazing to witness; your love is truly one of a kind," he said. I have never said "thank you" so many times. "But you need to keep rehabilitating him. Try aquatic therapy," he said. I drove home singing, "We made it, we really, really made it," to Brady, who panted and laughed with me in joint jubilation.

What Dr. Nate meant was Brady still needed to rebuild the muscles in his hind legs and haunches. Consider that he had spent almost 60 days without walking more than a few steps per day. But he had always been swim-team material. I researched aqua therapy facilities for canines, and found a unique facility near Brady's Retreat — our mountain home in the Berkshires — where we went for R&R.

I called the owner of Fitter Critters, Jody Chiquoine, and booked an appointment.

Fitter Critters was located in a cozy house, and the women working there were wearing swimsuits so we felt like we weren't at a medical facility, for once. They outfitted Brady with a lifejacket, and he jumped enthusiastically into the pool before they went through their procedure to coax him in. That made me smile, and he caught my eye to make sure I was watching. The therapists threw balls into one end of the pool, and coached Brady as he swam to fetch them. At regular intervals, the team would stop and palpate Brady's hind muscles under the water to increase range of motion and mobility. Brady smiled at me regularly with shining eyes. Then he would go back to being a comedian in the pool, hamming it up, as he scooped up the ball and tossed it to them. He made everyone laugh. This was the perfect symbiosis of fun and conditioning. My Brady was back.

The other appealing treatment they offered was an underwater treadmill. Hydro-treadmill therapy improves range of motion in compromised joints. It reduces the weight-bearing load of simple walking, so Brady could walk farther and longer while half-emerged. Fitter Critters told me that walking on an underwater treadmill helps patients with muscle atrophy gain muscle tone quickly. It also increases mobility, particularly because of the resistance that the viscose water creates.

The device looks exactly like a treadmill, but with four glass walls around it. The therapists would open up a door, secure Brady inside, and then fill up the container until it reached the bottom of his shoulders. When they turned the treadmill on, my job was to stand at one end and encourage Brady to start walking. He had jumped on my treadmill at home several times while I went to the bathroom, so he knew what to do.

Brady visited Fitter Critters three times a week for a combination of swimming therapy and walking on the underwater treadmill. He was soon wading through the deep snow in our Berkshires yard with confidence and strength. Everyone on Team Brady commented how strong and lithe he appeared in the photos I sent them. Brady had really made it.

"You willed Brady to live," Dr. Nate said to me, but that's not the whole story. Brady chose to fight. Brady related to me that he had vitality left in him, and I *listened* carefully to him, rather than exercising my right to euthanize him at will. I never once considered the possibility of euthanasia when he was sick. I believed in him, and I honored his dignity. We were warriors together in the medical fight. When I had told the kidney specialists at the emergency clinic that Brady was going to survive, they had looked at me like I was insane, but ultimately, Brady went home and broke all records. To this day, Dr. Whitney refers to Brady's case at least once a month with her patients experiencing acute renal failure; she explains that Brady's case shows what seems medically impossible can be achieved.

The theme that returns to me, as I contemplate the ingredients of Brady's healing, is the rhizomatic support and love coming from our various teams. Not only did we feel it from Team Brady at home with Dad, Janet, Kathy, and Arthur, but we felt it coming from our various teams of vets. Before our beloved Dr. Mike left Smith Ridge to take a teaching position in Florida, he told us to hold onto Dr. Nate because he was "one in a million." Dr. Mike and Dr. Nate had consulted about their special patient on the phone many times. We credit Dr. Mike for seeing us through those dark months at the emergency hospital, and for his treatment of Brady when he first came home from the hospital. He is also one in a million.

The last time I saw him, Dr. Mike looked me straight in the eyes and told me: "You need to write a book about Brady's story because it defies conventional veterinary wisdom." As Brady would underscore for me later, helping others was our mission, so writing a book about his healing—even though I was not well enough to write—went to the top of my priority list. Dr. Mike told me that veterinary students learn that the kidneys do not regenerate and that dogs with renal failure should be euthanized. Since the kidneys cannot generate new nephrons, they can no longer filter waste, thus there is no successful treatment for end-stage renal failure. Dr. Mike went on to say something that I will never forget:

"Brady is a miracle dog. He is one of the highlights of my career as a veterinarian." Brady's comeback from renal failure illustrates that love, intention, meditation, and the willingness to engage in mainstream and alternative healing modalities can produce medical miracles. That was something to celebrate, because, like Brady's renal failure and my chronic Lyme disease, there are things that we're told cannot be fought. Doctors had told me to acclimate to a new normal each time my symptoms worsened, but

Brady's recovery inspired me to keep fighting Lyme. The miracle consisted in the hope our teams brought us, and our resourcefulness in finding creative ways to keep fighting, even when people said there was no hope.

Chapter Fifteen
"Kerouacing" It Through the Southwest

When Dr. Nate recommended that Brady would do better during the winter in a warmer climate, I decided that since I wasn't teaching that semester, Brady and I would go on an extended road trip through the Southwest in search of a mixture of post-hospital freedom and catharsis, all while maintaining healthy kidneys. The exhilaration of Brady's recovery seemed to have bought me a rare respite from the Lyme symptoms that plagued me; I hadn't yet learned that adrenalin was deceptive for me. We set out to experience the pure joy of being on the road together.

A couple of weeks into the new year, I loaded my SUV with gear, including a dog bed and toys, hiking equipment, and a plug-in cooler with Brady's homemade meals. As I locked up the house for the winter, Brady bounded into the car with his old vigor and sat up in the front seat expectedly, as I made sure everything was secure. And just like that, Brady and I embarked on a road trip for several months.

We scooped D up from the Washington Dulles airport and drove to Charlotte to visit Debbie. Debbie's husband and two boys knew what Brady had overcome, and the role that Debbie had played, so they all greeted us with open arms. Brady knew that he was the guest of honor. He played with Debbie's dogs and licked everyone's hands, especially Debbie's. Debbie was overcome with joy to see how radiant Brady was. After a celebratory visit, we set off for Houston, with a few stops on the way.

Brady and I paused in Houston for a few months. We stayed with D in a calm wooded neighborhood, where Brady was pleased with his fenced-in yard and with the mild weather that enabled us to take long walks and meet other dogs in the neighborhood and parks. Brady and I both seemed restless, though. I was itching to embark on an epic road trip to express our new freedom. By March, we left Houston bound for all parts Southwest. I felt free-spirited and rebellious against the regimented medical regimen that had governed our lives ominously for the last several months. I loaded up the car, and my wildness was infectious. Brady knew something exciting was around the bend, and he traced my movements with his eyes.

We drove through West Texas bound for Marfa with Little Feat's song "Dixie Chicken" blasting and the sunroof open. Several hours later, we pulled up to the Hotel Paisano in Marfa, a funky, '50s-style hotel where Elizabeth Taylor and Rock Hudson lived during the filming of the Oscar-award-winning film *Giant*. Brady raced up the steps to our room and scoped out the square footage with his nose before he settled onto the outdoor balcony to observe the swimmers in the pool below.

We later ventured out to Planet Marfa, an open-air, dirt-floor bar where dogs roamed and an indie band performed under the stars. Brady came back to me from time to time to nudge my knee with his nose and lock eyes, but otherwise he frolicked with new canine friends in the bar.

At 5:00 a.m., Brady and I emerged from the Hotel Paisano with our bags. At the car, I paused and looked out. The darkness was illuminated by the ethereal stars that adumbrated the desert landscape. We clambered into the car, and I said the motto for the day out loud: "Sedona or bust." By mid-morning we were cruising through El Paso, Texas on the border of Juarez, Mexico, to the sounds of Emmy Lou Harris singing "Waltz Across Texas Tonight." I tried to accompany Emmy Lou, and even Brady groaned at this.

The Arizona welcome sign reassured me that we were getting closer to Sedona. Arizona meant that we got to see cacti, and stop in Tucson for lunch with Dad's childhood friend from Wellesley, Dick. Afterwards, we had ground to cover so I rolled along swiftly as I sang along with Mark Knopfler and Emmy Lou Harris singing "All the Roadrunning." The road to Sedona was quiet, the setting sun rendered the rusty canyons lavender, and a white new moon welcomed us. I was enchanted. We stopped at the Sedona Natural Grocers for supplies, and then we headed down a canyon to our home for the next several days. I told Brady, "We're almost here," and he scrambled around the backseat giddily, circling his bed several times.

I chose our home because it had a large fenced-in yard, which Brady was now gleefully exploring, nose first. As I unpacked, he would come back to nose me before returning to his new territory. In the morning, after a wholesome breakfast, we walked from our house to take an easy hike in the famous red rock formations of Sedona. It was a no-car day. Brady was thrilled—it was his first proper hike since the summer before his crisis.

I knew that hiking would build his muscles, so I vowed that we would hike every day that we were in Sedona. Brady looked to and fro, and it seemed as if he was gazing at the red rock formations jutting confidently in the sky before us. We were both transfixed by the mysterious outcroppings of rock that rose before us at every turn in russet, rust, and sumac.

The happy hiker in Sedona.

Before I knew it, he started swimming in a silvery stream that we were crossing. I caught up with him quickly. He was not going to contract leptospirosis again on my watch. He looked at me with sheer exuberance as he shook the flakes of red rock and water off. Those days were the best ones of the trip.

Far before we were ready to leave this magical place, we were packing up the car again, and venturing in the direction of the Grand Canyon. D was eager to join in on the fun, so he had flown into Phoenix and taken a bus to Sedona. I had yet another co-pilot, and this one could drive. There was a dusting of snow on the rocks on the morning that we left Sedona by way of a narrow, snowy canyon. Brady rolled and frolicked in the snow with abandon. He looked at me with his head cocked to the side as if to inquire, "How did snow get here, Michelle?"

Snow meant it might be cold at the Canyon. D and I wore down jackets and wool hats, but I marveled that Brady didn't require the extra fleece coat any longer. "Another milestone," I murmured to myself. It was surreal for me to look over the railing and see the panoramic layers of ochre, magenta, and rust in the distance against a periwinkle sky. Brady was mesmerized, too. He sat looking

139

over the railing for quite some time. "What a well-travelled German shepherd you are," I told Brady as we explored the Grand Canyon. "This is your gift. This is your reward for fighting so hard."

D and Brady at the Grand Canyon.

In early April, we disembarked in Aspen, where Brady marveled at the extreme climate change. One day we were hiking in Sedona's dry heat, and a few days later we were in snow-covered Aspen. For Brady, the snow cover magically appeared, and he seemed perplexed at this change, for he was accustomed to New England's distinct four seasons. He pawed the ground as if to find a reason for the abrupt temperature change. We stayed at a friend's condo at the Little Nell where Brady meandered out onto the ski slope and watched the lift going up and down. He would look up at me, and it seemed like he said:

"Can you really believe this is happening to us?"

"I can hardly believe it, Brady," I agreed. I crouched down and petted his back as I watched with him. Since I had spent much time in my youth in Aspen, I relaxed one layer deeper in my old stomping grounds alongside my family.

Aspen is a long way from Connecticut, so eventually, it was time to pack up the car and head for the Denver

Airport, to send D back to Houston. Brady barked when D slung his bag over his shoulder and left the car, even though there had been numerous farewells. Brady and I continued north to Boulder, where we would rest our heads for a week.

The entire town was coterminous with our credo of freedom, with its mountaineers, gentrified hippies, and free-spirited folks. While we were in Boulder, Brady visited a holistic vet to get his customary fluids. His levels were holding up, and the vet was amazed at his story. "You really are a miracle dog," she told him. I reveled in this great affirmation of our medical treatments, our meditations, our positive attitude, our unwavering dedication to Brady's wellness, and in the power of interspecies love. I started to feel a stirring to write about it from a philosophical perspective, and this lingered in my mind on our walks.

I was eager to show Brady some of my favorite hikes in Boulder's front range; I thought that we could always turn around if it was too arduous for us. He was so athletic and fit that we hiked to the summit and down, with me trailing behind. This was one of the highlights of our trip. No one would have believed that he had just come back from the brink of death. On our last morning in Boulder, Brady knew it was time to travel again, and he curled up in nap mode in the backseat. How comfortable he looked, confident that his girl had the navigation under control. We pointed our compass in the direction of Nashville, homeward bound.

After stops with old friends in Nashville and Asheville, I explained to Brady that we would be driving to Vermont the next day. If we had both died the day that we returned home, it all would have been worth it. I had no regrets, and we were living according to the principle of *carpe diem,* one that I had always loved. While I drove, I pondered some of the more profound philosophical questions that my relationship with Brady stirred. I knew it was time to contend with philosophy.

CHAPTER SIXTEEN
"BUT BRADY IS JUST A DOG": CONTENDING WITH PHILOSOPHY

Although D went to extraordinary lengths to care for Brady, he grappled with the way I prioritized Brady above all else. To be fair, Brady's medical treatment was extraordinary. In addition to his nearly two-month stay at the emergency hospital in Connecticut, and his emergency surgery in Wisconsin, Brady's post-leptospirosis care was extensive and expensive. Even though Brady survived acute renal failure, he required both IV fluids and subcutaneous fluids on a regular basis in the chronic renal failure phase. Furthermore, Brady took pricey Chinese herbs daily that Dr. Nate prescribed to preserve his remaining kidney function, and Dr. Nate gave Brady frequent acupuncture and laser therapy treatments. Making Brady's homemade kidney diet was a very time-consuming and costly procedure, to say the least. D looked at Brady's exorbitant expenses (that would have been a small fraction if he had agreed to pet health insurance early on) and said repeatedly: "But Brady is just a dog."

D's tone seemed to accentuate the word 'just,' sardonically, as if he were implying that because Brady was not a human, I should not have expended such time, care, and finances to maintain Brady's health and wellbeing. Conversely, D would call from work to ask: "Has Brady eaten? How much? How are his fluid treatments progressing?" He got blustery with me if I reported that I couldn't cajole Brady into eating. Thus, D's statement that "Brady is just a dog" doesn't mean that he wrote Brady off as unworthy of care and treatment. He simply wrestled philosophically with the idea of what a dog is, and what a dog merits.

There are surely readers who sympathize with these quandaries. The reader may ask: "Why didn't she just put him down?" It is, after all, within my legal rights as a so-called animal owner to euthanize my animal at any time that I decide to end his life. I waived my right to euthanize Brady at my whim, though. Instead, I honored his needs, and I met them to the best of my ability.

Brady was combatting an illness with all of his strength when I made the decision to support him through leptospirosis; he was also a young dog at five and a half years old. Furthermore, through the tool of animal communication, Brady conveyed that he wanted to keep fighting. My human family agreed with my decision to save Brady. Janet argued that saving Brady was no different than saving a person. It was a given for her that D and I would have allocated all of our financial, emotional, and physical resources to saving Brady. Dad reiterated that: "One does whatever it takes to help family members through challenging times, so that's what we all did for Brady." He made *no distinction* between human and nonhuman animal family members. I concur, though the thorny questions I have posited innumerable times are: "How do I frame this philosophically?" "Is it possible to, or does it fall into the category of what French psychoanalyst Jacques Lacan would call the *insaisissable*?"

Everyone is clambering to get it "right" about nonhuman animals today. It has become a minefield to write about the subject of the nonhuman animal, because everyone from animal rights philosophers and ethics philosophers to posthumanists and bio-ethicists have developed sophisticated theories that make it daunting to add one's thoughts to the mix.

Even the acclaimed scholar of animal studies Donna Haraway writes about her qualms broaching philosophical questions about nonhuman animals: "I am afraid to start writing what I have been thinking about all of this, because I will get it wrong — emotionally, intellectually, and morally — and the issue is consequential."[25] I used to be afraid of what academia would think of me when I wrote about the language of Dog, but based on my empirical experiences with Brady, I have come to terms about being an outlier.

I'd like to provide an alternative to Western philosophy's theories on the nonhuman animal and unravel the opposition between human and animal that relegates the animal to a state bereft of consciousness, spirit, reason, and communication. My conversations with Brady put me in a unique place to do so, and this is the moment to do it, since the multidisciplinary field of animal studies is challenging centuries of anthropocentric dogmatism. The humanities, sciences, social sciences, and arts are addressing the ethical and philosophical elements of human and animal interactions. Bioethics and biomedicine are taking up the question of the animal in groundbreaking ways.

Contemporary philosopher Matthew Calarco writes that philosophers and scientists in animal studies "share the conviction that the question of the animal should be seen as one of the central issues" of our time.[26] Donna Haraway writes in *Cyborg Manifesto* that by the late 20th century, the boundary between animal and human has been completely breached, at least in the American scientific community. She goes on to write that nothing really separates animal and human anymore, not even the language tool argument, and that humans don't even feel the need for such a separation anymore.[27] Haraway's observation that barriers have been effaced even in regards to language paves the way for narratives on the animal and human relationship such as this one, in which the nonhuman animal (Brady) communicates complex ideas as a unique being in his own right. But philosophy has wildly divergent theories on the animal human relationship that are not nearly as progressive as Haraway's are.

Contractarian philosopher Jan Narveson would frame my decision to save Brady in the context of moral contracts. Narveson states that companion animals should be treated well solely for the benefit of their human owners, to avoid causing them pain and suffering.[28] We only have a moral duty to other humans, since, as Narveson argues, animals aren't capable of grasping the concept of morality. In this case, D could have argued, "Of course Brady is just a dog, yet we should not upset Michelle, who loves him. Therefore, we should treat him with kindness." I reject the contractarian theory, since, given Brady's natural proclivities to protect me, I believe Brady felt that *he* was the one with a moral duty to take care of me.

I could have responded to D with a defensive riposte, a riff on the word 'just,' saying "Brady may be just a dog, and I may be just a human, but all beings defy these conventional rubrics, and we refuse to be limited by them." Or I could have responded, "No Just(ification) needed, for the action of showing something to be right or reasonable is not necessary here; Brady and I have a relationship that is beyond justification." I do not feel that I brought (just) ice to Brady, nor did I feel that it was *just* behavior to save him based on a problematic animal rights argument. Was Brady subjected to *just*, or morally right and fair treatment, even though he is "just a dog?"

In fact, thoughts of morality and justice never once entered my mind when I rushed Brady to the emergency hospital. My mother taught me to treat our fellow animal beings—including animals we didn't know and companion animals—the way we would treat our family members and friends. I didn't fail to notice that she treated

145

me and Joy with the same patience, respect, and love. Mom acknowledged Joy's intelligence, personality, and humor, and she spoke to Joy in complete sentences the way that she spoke to me. I never felt that Joy was subservient to me, even though I wasn't fluent in Dog yet. My mother was operating under the principle of what moral philosophy would call a special obligation.

Special obligations are owed to those with whom we are in a special relationship, whether they are friends, family, or colleagues. Ethics philosopher Diane Jeske summarizes the ongoing argument about including animals in the special obligations category. Americans spend small fortunes providing medical care for their animal companions, and lavish time, attention, and love on them. But can we really have special obligations to nonhuman animals? If not, how can we possibly justify the resources expended on companion animals, given the amount of human suffering in the world?[29]

Jeske is asking how we can make a promise to an animal if that promise cannot be heard, and her reference to justifying the exorbitant costs of companion animal health care belies a humanistic belief that humans are more important than animals.

We can make promises to animals if we take animal communication into account, in which case the animal can hear. Debbie affirmed this for me when she relayed a powerful story about a lion she worked with at the wild animal rescue facility Tigers for Tomorrow in Attalla, Alabama.

A lion named Kazuma was rescued from a man who kept him confined in the back of a small pickup truck. Kazuma's muscles were severely atrophied from being immobilized, but the rescuers wanted Kazuma to walk into a tiny transport cell by himself, without drugs. Debbie asked Kazuma if he would agree to get into the transport cell.

"Kazuma, all of your needs will be taken care of in your new home," she promised. Kazuma told Debbie that he wanted to make the journey to his new home. He stood up and walked into the crate on his own accord, without sedation. A promise was made to Kazuma, which he understood. He acted accordingly, one might even say with reason, even though the transport vehicle was even smaller than his cramped quarters.

Kazuma went on to live a fuller life at the expansive Tigers for Tomorrow preserve, just as Debbie had promised. Through the language of Dog, I promised Brady that we would fight his illness together, and he heard me. If we fail to bring animal communication to the fore, we will be asking inadequate philosophical questions such as whether we can make promises to animals and whether they can make reasonable decisions. Philosophy, though, would place a red flag next to the word "reason" in conjunction with the animal.

In his provocative novella *The Lives of Animals*, constructed as a fictional lecture series on animal rights, Nobel-prize-winning novelist J.M. Coetzee contextualizes the animal in Western philosophy: "[…] animals, lacking reason, cannot understand the universe, but have simply to follow its rules blindly," which "proves that, unlike man, they are part of it but not part of its being: that man is godlike, animals thing-like."[30]

Throughout the history of Western philosophy, dogs and animals at large have been dismissed as mere machines and puppets. The word "puppy" even derives from "puppet," as if a puppy is a doll-like object that is not rational, is unable to think, and lacks consciousness. In the 17th century, French philosopher René Descartes' famous dictum "I think therefore I am" resulted in a devastating critique on animals that had staying power largely until the late 20th century. As a human, I think, therefore I exist, but animals do not think, so therefore they do not exist. Descartes writes derisively that the animal is a mere machine, leaving no room for animal consciousness in Cartesian thought. If D were speaking in Cartesian vernacular, he would have said, "But Brady is just a *machine!*"

Yet in 1789, 150 years after Descartes wrote *Discourse on Method*, British utilitarian philosopher Jeremy Bentham published his *Introduction to the Principles of Morals and Legislation* at a time when revolutionary ideals were spreading throughout Europe and America. I find his response to the deeply disturbing Cartesian argument for denying an animal's worth to be extraordinary, and it has shaped not only my own position, but also the positions of those philosophers I respect the most.

Although Bentham's powerful commentary on the animal is embedded within a dense text on juridical law, his comments and questions are revolutionary for his time, and they're still controversial. To reach Bentham's thoughts on the animal, one must wade through 300 pages of his reflections on the penal code to get to private ethics.[31] It's only the most dedicated reader who will find Bentham's comments on the animal, placed in a lengthy footnote. One could argue that Bentham's comments on the animal are relegated to a footnote because they were deemed not important enough to be included in the body of the text. Even if he found them important, their placement in the footnote may make the reader feel that it's not to us to drag them out for inspection. I disagree.

Bentham protests that animals' interests have been neglected, and they have been degraded into a class of *"things."* Things is italicized, as if to emphasize Bentham's distaste at this Cartesian designation. He hopes for the day when animals may acquire rights — making him an early forerunner of the complicated animal rights movement. For Bentham, "[…] the question is not, can they reason, nor can they talk, but can they suffer? Why should the law refuse its protection to any sensitive being?"[32] For Bentham — and this is the extraordinary revolution against the stronghold of Cartesian thought — commensurability between the animal and the human lies not with the faculties of speech or reason, but with the common denominator of suffering. When Bentham asks the resounding question "Can they suffer?" he acknowledges the *joint* vulnerability that humans and animals share, and he expresses compassion for that vulnerability. And, I'll return to this vulnerability soon, as it relates to the critical concept of shared finitude that I want to dwell on, to stamp out the possibility of saying: "just a dog;" it also raises the question: "and who do you think you — the human — are?"

Bentham's utilitarianism provided much fodder for 20th-century animal rights philosophers and activists.[33] Yet there's no organized protection for animals that provides binding support for their welfare.[34] Bentham's call for the establishment of animal rights has not yet been achieved, and it comes with problems. Many leading contemporary theorists reject Bentham's arguments on the premise that utilitarians always privilege human rights over animal rights.

In utilitarianism, duty is determined by the comparative value of consequences. Although there may be an allowance for duty to an animal, the duty to the human is always greater within the utilitarian branch of humanism. I'm running up against a sticky issue in philosophy about moral standing when I contest the "just a dog" comment. It seems that if I say, "Brady is most certainly not 'just a dog,' and I am determined to alleviate his suffering," I'll be criticized for bringing up the humanistic moral issue, as if the degree to which Brady suffered paled in comparison to the importance of say, my own suffering. But I don't think there's any comparison to be made between Brady's pain and various levels of human suffering, and that stance denies humans their once normative Cartesian superiority.

Leading posthumanist scholar Cary Wolfe sums up this argument best in a January 2017 *New York Times* interview with Natasha Lennard:

> But the problem with how rights discourse addresses this problem — in animal rights philosophy, for example — is that animals end up having some kind of moral standing insofar as they are diminished versions of us: that is to

say, insofar as they are possessed of various characteristics such as the capacity to experience suffering—and not just brute physical suffering but emotional duress as well—that we human beings possess more fully. And so we end up reinstating a normative form of the moral-subject-as-human that we wanted to move beyond in the first place.[35]

The way Wolfe describes this problem from a posthumanist perspective—that dismantles the placement of the human at the center of the world—blows the idea of "just a dog" up, for it acknowledges that the suffering that Brady experienced in the emergency hospital was legitimate in its own right without being a lesser form of human suffering. In his pivotal book, *What is Posthumanism?* Wolfe explains that posthumanism rejects the "anthropological drama" associated with humanism and it "decenters the human," which leads to the "necessity of new theoretical paradigms."[36] Within the realm of new paradigms is the recognition, as Wolfe explains it in the interview with Lennard of what "nonhuman animals" really are:

So on the other hand, what one wants to do is to find a way of valuing nonhuman life not because it is some diminished or second-class form of the human, but because the diversity and abundance of life is to be valued for what it is in its own right, in its difference and uniqueness. An elephant or a dolphin or a chimpanzee isn't worthy of respect because it embodies some normative form of the "human" plus or minus a handful of relevant moral characteristics. It's worthy of respect for reasons that call upon us to come up with another moral vocabulary, a vocabulary that starts by acknowledging that whatever it is we value ethically and morally in various forms of life, it has nothing to do with the biological designation of "human" or "animal."[37]

I concur with Wolfe that "…the question of the human versus animal is a woefully inadequate philosophical tool to make sense of the amazing diversity of different forms of life, how they experience the world and how they should be treated."[38] I look beyond whether one labels Brady merely a dog, or an animal, because I'm not interested in pursuing a discussion on the binary between humans and nonhuman animals that has created such divisive distinctions. I, too, think it's an outdated means of philosophical investigation, and it doesn't take the advancements in animal communication into account that present a radically new theoretical paradigm (probably too radical for most of the thinkers I'm citing in this chapter).

Moving past the humanistic perspective's shortcomings, I want to return to the force of Bentham's argument regarding the criterion of suffering, for Bentham's powerful and *empathetic* question "Can they suffer?" is integral to the basis of my argument that sees suffering as a lynchpin in the philosophical argument about "just a dog." When I read Bentham's words "can they" suffer" in the context of posthumanism, I'm taken back to my haunting experience with Brady at the emergency hospital. I was witnessing the being that I loved the most suffer — a being we would call a nonhuman animal — who I had long called my interspecies soul mate. I suffered as I watched his helplessness, but I put my suffering aside as I witnessed his vulnerability. I privileged his condition over mine. As we lived through a nightmare narrative with the specter of death at our shoulder, I didn't dwell on the incomprehensibility of that. Rather, I was acutely aware of my compassion for Brady as a unique being.[39] My thoughts, even while Brady and I were in the thick of this horror, reminded me of a book by my one of my favorite philosophers, one that I had even written about in an academic context. On the long leg of the road trip from Colorado to Connecticut, I contemplated what Derrida had to say about nonhuman animals.

In the most powerful theory on the animal human

relationship that I have ever read, *The Animal that Therefore I am*, the formidable late French philosopher Jacques Derrida writes that he sees his cat as an irreplaceable being: "Nothing can ever take away from me the certainty that what we have here is an existence that refuses to be conceptualized."[40] Derrida refers to the unique identity that I recognize in Brady as the "unsubstitutable singularity" of each nonhuman animal.[41] Therefore, Derrida is well-equipped to understand what was at stake in Bentham's profound footnote. Derrida states in an interview that all of his efforts throughout his career consist in "questioning the self-interested misrecognition of what is called the Animal in general, and the way in which these interpret the border between Man and Animal."[42] In a posthumanist vein of thought, Derrida raises the stakes by stating that the issue of the animal is passing through a critical phase, it's not only a duty, or an obligation, but it's a necessity that no one can escape.

No one has interpreted Bentham with more acuity or sensitivity than Derrida has, so I quote him here in the following powerful statement that I want to dwell on:

> Can they suffer?" amounts to asking "Can they *not be able*?" And what of this inability [*impouvoir*]? What of the vulnerability felt on the basis of this inability? What is this nonpower at the heart of power? [...]Mortality resides there, as the most radical means of thinking the finitude that we share with animals, the mortality that belongs to the very finitude of life, to the experience of compassion, to the possibility of sharing this nonpower, the possibility of this impossibility, the anguish of this vulnerability, and the vulnerability of this anguish.[43]

What resonates with me most about Derrida's interpretation of Bentham's question regarding suffering is that it brings out the vulnerability of the animal, the way it is not able, and the way that humans and animals share this finitude and vulnerability; the compassion Derrida evokes is palpable. Nowhere in the history of philosophy do I find words that resonate with my life experience more than how Derrida describes radically rethinking finitude. When others thought Brady was dying, I had to keep displacing that thought, for I know that there is no referent for death. But something transformative transpired at that precarious place where life hung in the balance: I witnessed not only Brady's strength to fight, but simultaneously, I witnessed his helplessness. But it was the vulnerability that came from Brady's "not being able" as Derrida puts it that troubled me the most, that was entirely different from the vulnerability I felt given what I knew about finitude and Grief. It was our joint vulnerability in the sense of Derrida's *impouvoir*, within the context of his formidable statements that lead to the question I would have posed to D: "if Brady is just a dog, then *who are you*? Are you sure?" But the recognition of shared finitude and vulnerability only goes so far because Brady had to rely on my ability to provide him with medical attention, and there are countless nonhuman animals who have no one to fend for them the way I did for Brady, which I was constantly aware of.

Writing about finitude brings me to the philosophical consideration of love between animals and human beings. Why did I do what I did for Brady? It was also out of love. When one of Derrida's students, filming him, asked him to speak on the subject of love in philosophy, Derrida laughed at the suggestion. He wouldn't touch the question of love, saying that he would be talking in clichés. But what Derrida did write about is the concept of finitude and friendship, which implicitly involves love. In *Memoirs for Paul de Man*, Derrida argues that "there is no friendship without this knowledge of finitude."[44] Finitude and mourning, and dare I say love, are interrelated. To be aware of finitude, and to mourn, is to have someone who is worthy of love.

I'll take this question of love on since my soul mate was a dog, but never just a dog.

Returning to the citation I shared earlier from Kundera's novel *The Unbearable Lightness of Being*, I quote it again to underscore that it is not uncomplicated to love a dog. The narrator describes the character Tereza's love for her dog Karenin:

"The love she bore her dog made her feel cut off, isolated. With a sad smile, she told herself that she needed to hide it more than she would an affair. People are indignant at the thought of someone loving a dog."[45] This stance of indignance and concealment reinforces the longstanding "just a dog" attitude. Immanuel Kant suggested that tender feelings for animals could inspire humans to be more humane towards humans, which reinforces the humanism argument we have already left behind, because "tender feelings," don't account for what Tereza clearly experienced as unconditional love. I propose the simple notion: unconditional love for the other being has lessons for us, it expands our willingness to take extraordinary measures to provide for the other, and it helps us overcome our skepticism about the nature of the other being, which I'm leading up to.

If I loved Brady unconditionally, without the constraint of conditions—if nothing could diminish the strength and quality of my love for him—and I argue that he also loved me unconditionally, then how can animals and humans be incommensurable? I'm simplifying things, but that unconditional love made me vulnerable and even more aware of his finitude. But people have doubted this love. Some people have conjectured that I loved Brady so profoundly because I didn't have any children at that time, but Brady could never be a place marker substituting for a human's love. Philosophy has had a hard time grappling with love between humans and animals, even on the level of friendship.

Medieval philosopher Thomas Aquinas maintained in *Summa Theologica* that friendship between animals and humans is impossible because animals are not rational beings. The millions of humans who have friendships with nonhuman animals would balk against this preposterous claim. *Being with one another,* being in *community,* as fellow beings, should not be underestimated. Brady's various communiqués demonstrated to me that he was able to reason, which for me, broke down the Berlin Wall of Cartesian thought dividing the human and the nonhuman animal. It permitted him to express his love for me. I say that not only is friendship possible, but animals can love humans, as humans can love animals.

What I am arguing here is that love is a rational concept. As French philosopher Jean-Luc Nancy puts it, "it is love that receives and deploys the experience of thinking."[46] Based on reason, my love for Brady cannot be characterized as an excess of sentimentality, affect, or irrationality. My love for Brady is based on the Platonic ideal of *eros,* or a higher order love that is non-physical, and recognizes the transcendent beauty of the other. My love for Brady draws from Aristotle's explanation of *philia* in Book VII of his Nicomachean ethics, which loosely translates into genuine fondness and affection for the other. The love I have for Brady is most like *agape* love that synthesizes elements of *eros* and *philia,* for it is an absolute love that is not based on conditions. My love for Brady is a higher order love that is axiomatic and irreducible, and that kind of love can transcend species.

When it came time to write our narrative, I asked Brady if he had a message to share with the reader about our unconditional love. He had an eloquent one, and I quote it for you verbatim, as Debbie transcribed his dictation:

We are all alike because we all have the same need and deep desire: to feel love. All beings require this to nourish them. Love is the one thing that cannot be swapped out for something else. Love is a term that is used loosely by humans. There is only one true form of love, and that is unconditional love. That is to love without reservation or conditions. Unconditional love becomes the light that raises the person or animal to a new level of awareness. This is the true quest of all living things. Love does not come disguised as jealousy, passion, fear, anger or obsession. It does not turn on and off like a light. It burns eternally, and it is pure and simple. Don't be fooled by imitations, because that is part of the puzzle of life. Figuring out where the imitations are. I love my human unconditionally and she me. We have found the missing piece to our puzzle. What is your missing piece?

Brady's message defines unconditional love in a way that not even I was able to do, and his definition of love as pure, unadulterated, and authentic is sublime. He is the one who taught me what unconditional love is, because it did feel like my humans sometimes turned their love on and off like a light when it came to me. Brady's message leads me to an idea that changes the stakes of the human animal relationship debate: if the pursuit of love is a common denominator between species, then love supersedes the faculty of reason and the faculty of speech.

As a mere thing in Descartes' dictum, Brady does not think, feel, speak, or reason, therefore he absolutely could not have transmitted this message, and I am a charlatan for attributing it to Brady. Even in the field of animal studies, this would be considered far out. In addition to these problems, much could be said here about the problem of translation, about the issue of Debbie as translator, as the one who takes dictation. Philosophical questions will crop up about the usage of language here, but for now, I'll put aside these questions about Debbie's task as a translator as material for another project. Based on the consistently accurate messages Debbie has communicated to me from Brady, I find Brady's message to be authentic. For me, it tears down the animal-human barrier that Western philosophy has cemented from Descartes to Heidegger, yet this does not solve the problem of your doubt as a reader.

Brady's message revolutionizes the human and animal relationship by smudging the line of otherness between animal and human. It bridges the gap in speech, reason, and feeling. J. Allen Boone would have understood it, based on his conversations with Strongheart. Yet some will think that it must be a hoax. Through Debbie, Brady has said that most people don't see him for who he truly is because humans have a limited view of dogs and their character. He appreciates that I see beyond the stereotypes that humans have attributed to the form of a dog.

What if you were to trust me? What if you were to trust that this message originated from Brady, as he transmitted it to Debbie and me? What if we were to find a solution to our skepticism and put this humanism to rest that downplays what an animal is?

The late American philosopher Stanley Cavell puts forth a formidable solution to the problem of how to account for the other. Here, we want to know how we can account for the nonhuman animal as "other." How can we account for the possibility that the animal speaks? How can we acknowledge the animal? Cavell offers some of my favorite philosophical sentences of all time: "[…] the problem is to *recognize* myself as denying another, to understand that I carry chaos in myself. Here is the scandal of skepticism with respect to the existence of others; I am the scandal."[47] In other words, who are you, who am I to judge the existence of the other, to judge the limits of the other?

In this denial, the human is the scandal of skepticism — the human reinforces the problem of otherness by putting the nonhuman animal in the category of the outsider, the marginalized. What if you were to acknowledge Brady's transmission as the message of an evolved canine being? What would that mean? Perhaps it would mean becoming open to the magic of the animal world, acknowledging our "radical unabashed ignorance of things," as Cavell calls it, beyond the limited five senses.

There are many failed relationships between dogs and humans, though, in which dogs are cemented as the "other," in an "us" versus "them" relationship, such as Hélène Cixous's story of Fips that I related earlier. Cixous ruminated on her communication breakdown with her childhood dog Fips for decades before she was able to write about it in philosophical terms that recognized Fips' depth. It was the remembrance of the failure that led her to a retroactive epiphany about the potential of the human-animal rapport, or shared *humanimality*, "my dog was something else, [he was] much more than I and I do not know what a dog is nor what being a dog is."[48] As an adult, Cixous avoids being what Cavell calls the scandal of skepticism, for she sees beyond Fips' otherness. Fips was not "just a dog," as Cixous came to realize, yet how can one avoid a 40-year misunderstanding, resolved only through a retrospective philosophical realization?

The communication breakdown between Fips and Cixous represents countless stories of animals and humans failing to understand one another throughout the world: this is what happens when we do not speak the language of Dog and we expect dogs to speak solely in human language. As a result of such dire misunderstandings, many people abandon their dogs at shelters when they reach communication impasses. In the United States, 3.9 million dogs, or five percent of the entire companion dog population, will enter animal shelters every year. Some 1.3 million dogs are relinquished by their human caretakers, and 2.6 million dogs enter the shelters as strays with unknown narratives. This is the scandal of skepticism, per Cavell.

I could have easily given up and reinforced the age-old human-animal boundary, yet I intuited that this barrier was *meant to be crossed.* Debbie opened the door with her unconventional language classes, so I could listen to Brady and learn the language of Dog. As Dad contended, "The relationship between dogs and humans becomes multidimensional when you can communicate like you have been able to do with Brady." I asked Brady what he thought of our ability to break through the communication barrier, and he replied: "I'm lucky because Michelle takes the time to know me. How can other people get along because they can't hear their animals? People don't stop long enough to listen and hear their animals." That's how we get mired in the scandal of skepticism and end up casting off dogs as mere machines.

Brady's comments remind me of the question fictional author Elizabeth Costello posits in J.M. Coetzee's *The Lives of Animals.* "Do we really understand the universe better than animals do?"[49] Based on what Professor Brady has shown me, I think it is impudent of us to think so.

Philosophy and science are unable to make further progress understanding animal beings without learning a new language, one that relies not on ears and tongues, but on the mind. The notion of animals and humans as fellow beings becomes plausible when humans can communicate through the language of Dog in a post-linguistic space.

Language can be an unwieldy tool to say the least. Entire movements of theory and philosophy from semiotics to post-structuralism have focused on the difficulties in interpreting language between humans, which I can't begin to account for here, and animals haven't fared well in most of these theories. In her compelling account of her relationship with a goose, *Solitary Goose,* Sydney Landon Plum writes: "Language has always been a problem in writing the lives of animals, because mankind has established a hierarchy of consciousness with language — making (the kind that we do) near or at the pinnacle. We assume that without language there is no story to tell."[50]

We have placed undue emphasis on the faculty of speech in order to find animals lacking, yet this notoriously ambiguous faculty has limits. As Stanley Cavell famously wrote in a passage that I have underlined many times in *The Claim of Reason,* "We begin to feel, or ought to, terrified that maybe language (and understanding, and knowledge) rests upon very shaky foundations — a thin net over an abyss."[51]

Debbie has said to me, based on her experience talking to animals in thousands of conversations that "skepticism is healthy, but it limits us. We are so limited to think that speaking is the only way of communicating. There is a communication that cannot be seen or heard.

It's so efficient. It's so much more efficient than the verbal word." Who are we humans to claim that we are superior because we have the language that we speak?

Fortunately, not all of the philosophical humans think this. In a groundbreaking interview with Derrida, Jean-Luc Nancy asked him what happens to language in the shift from man to animal. Derrida famously responded that he had issues with the idea that man is the only one who speaks, and he went on to say:

> Of course, if one defines language in such a way that it is reserved for what we call man, what is there to say? But if one reinscribes language in a network of possibilities that do not merely encompass it but mark it irreducibly from the inside, everything changes.... These possibilities or necessities, without which there would be no language, *are themselves not only human.*[52]

Derrida includes scientific evidence about the sophistication of animal languages within his list of possibilities, and I posit that one day, the language of Dog learned through what's known as animal communication could be on that list.

Wolfe sees the work of animal studies as: "fundamentally rethinking the question of what knowledge is," and "examining our assumptions about who the knowing subject can be."[53] Conduct your own empirical explorations, listen to what the nonhuman animals have to say, and see how that changes your relation to them and to yourself.

I am not claiming Brady has more standing, that he transcended being "just a dog" merely because he has similar faculties to the ones that I have (including communication and language), rather I'm arguing that through the language of Dog, I can listen to how he is different and autonomous in relation to me. As I learned from Brady, his perspective is sagacious, hilarious, and reasonable, and it differs from that of other animal beings. Brady was here to educate me and my fellow humans, as an ambassador for the canine voices that have not been heard, for the subaltern canine. I posit that we let the animals help teach us to cross this frontier. Listen.

CHAPTER SEVENTEEN
A LETTER FROM BRADY

The day after we visited Debbie and her family, she sent me a letter from Brady, which I share now that the philosophical context has been broached:

"Hi Miche,

I was going to bed last night and took a moment to thank Brady for being such a gentleman with the children and other dogs, and I told him what a pleasure it was to have him in our home. I told him he could write you a letter if he wanted, and he began dictating it to me right away. He had a lot to say so I hopped out of bed and began to write it down. I knew if I didn't, we would have lost that moment. He was so excited, and here is what he shared."

Brady frequently suggested to Debbie that I should be writing down what he said. One time he said impishly: "Tell her to keep a notepad by her bed because I have been sending her a stream of messages to write down. These are good quotes." Brady always had a wealth of information to share with Debbie, too. He did on this particular night, and I pondered over what he had to say for a long while. It took me even longer to decide whether the reader would be ready for such an extraordinary communiqué coming from a German shepherd.

I want you to know that we are a meeting of the minds

and hearts. I say this because many of the things you have done that I have contributed to. In my recent health scare, it was nothing more than a way for you to trust in the unknown, in something that can't be seen, but can be believed. This is my gift to you, a way for you to know that the power of love, of belief, and of not surrendering to fear can manifest great changes and miracles. We will continue on our path together as I have a second chance at life as I see it. You fulfilled the purpose of my teachings as now we can progress to our true purpose, which is helping others. You see our souls intersect at places others do not. We are to work together in a way that has not been done before. We don't waste time, we want to get business done, but we do it together and with the love we share, it never feels like business. And when I say business, I mean reaching our goals and our higher purpose. For after all, that is why we are here. But make no mistake. We are impacting others, either directly or indirectly… all we come into contact with, we impact. This is not a statement of ego, but one of knowing our direct purpose. It is to teach others in a way that has not been done before. And for that I am grateful to you. You have always chosen the road that may not have been widely used to get to where you need to go. For this I am grateful. You are a fearless warrior for my welfare, and for this I am grateful. You want for me more than you want for you, and I want you to know that I want for you more than I want for me. I guess we are alike.

Although Brady's letter did not astonish me, I realize that the reader may view the epistolary element of our rapport with incredulity. How could a canine expound on such profound concepts?

Animals may also be philosophical. While I was writing this book, I visited Debbie again in North Carolina to interview her about some of the more profound conversations that she had with Brady—conversations that the reader may struggle to accept. Debbie told me that she felt humbled by him, as her equal and teacher. "I am honored to communicate with a wise soul," Debbie said.

Debbie was skeptical when she first heard animals speaking to her, but animals taught her that we are all souls in these physical bodies with much to communicate.

Perhaps this is why dogs and humans are so attracted to one another—perhaps they sense this greater means of communicating and a greater purpose in their interactions?

Yet scientists are not so sure at all about the legitimacy of animal communication. As ethologists Raymond Coppinger and Mark Feinstein write in *How Dogs Work:* "Some researchers pin their hopes on the possibility that animal communication systems are more meaningful than we think they are and that decoding the 'language' of a dog, for instance, might open the window a bit. The sad truth is that we don't really have much to go on yet if we want to know whether dogs are conscious."[54] Although I realize that scientifically, there is no proof of animal communication's legitimacy, I present this material as one who has experienced it firsthand. I *acknowledge* it without being able to present a more scientific explanation. But I did ask Debbie about her methodology.

Some of my questions for Debbie pertained to the letter I just quoted from Brady. I asked her to describe how the message came to her from Brady in such complete thoughts and sentences. "How can I explain to readers in a way that they might understand that this is not coming from you?"

Debbie said that when she is working with an animal, she receives their concentration of energy, which they trust her to translate. "I will sense things; I will feel things. It comes through so fast that I just write, and I don't even know what I'm writing because it's just coming through me as a conduit. My intention is to get the message across as accurately as possible. I don't want to have any of my own thought processes affecting the animal."

I realize that what I am recounting in these pages may be new to some readers, but I'm hardly breaking ground. I'm not the first to witness that animals transcend the qualities and faculties traditionally ascribed to them, to recognize that animals have profound depth that goes beyond what can be explained from the current scientific perspective. I read articles and books on animals often, and what I have noticed is a pattern of avoiding explanations of the "beyond" or that which we cannot explain through the dominant five senses. Let's go beyond the current catchphrase "there is something beyond" in animals. Most experts and authors are unsure how to enter through the portal, and so they leave it at that. I hope this book helps others to enter the beyond and see what's there.

Narratives and memoirs of relationships between species are far more prevalent than they were when Montaigne was marveling at the abilities of his animals to communicate. Personal narrative and philosophy can come together to form a 21st-century love story that effaces the implied limitations between animals and humans' capabilities.

Mark Rowlands writes in *The Philosopher and the Wolf* about an extrasensory experience he had while building a cairn over his recently deceased wolf companion's grave.[55] He haphazardly piled rocks to form the cairn while in a stupor of grief, until he noticed that the cairn was built in the same shape as his beloved Brenin. He doesn't provide a philosophical explanation, nor does he treat the ramifications of this phenomenon, but he knows he witnessed something supernatural.

It isn't enough just to name an animal's capacity as "supernatural," though. Likewise, biologist Stacey O'Brien wrote a bestselling memoir *Wesley the Owl* about the extraordinary rapport she had with her owl companion.[56] O'Brien clearly communicated with Wesley, and these powerful exchanges led her to write that we are on the brink of a new understanding about animal communication. O'Brien concludes by acknowledging that we are in the dark ages about the spiritual, intellectual, and emotional capacities of animals. Rowlands and O'Brien don't delve into analyzing their experiences that took them beyond the conventional boundaries of what animals are capable of, but as they call for an exploration of the true capacity of animals, they end their narratives without embarking on what the details mean. As I'm writing about animal communication with Brady, I'm probing it from all angles to understand not only him, but what all the animals really have to say.

Yet scholars across the humanities and scientists are reluctant to broach the subject of animal communication through telepathy because it doesn't appear to be rooted in science or in concrete empirical methods. There is a general avoidance of relying on one's intuition within academic fields. Indeed, it's frowned upon.

Of course, there are exceptions. In an essay on her experiences with African baboons, scientist Barbara Smuts writes that she communicated with a female baboon by "silently sending friendliness her way."[57] To the surprise of Smuts, the baboon approached her and embraced her in her "long ape arms." This extraordinary experience prompted her to adopt a dog upon her return from Africa, who has given Smuts the "opportunity to experience a joyful intersubjectivity that transcends species boundaries." A Stanford-trained psychologist and an anthropologist with a background in neuroscience, Smuts is exactly the sort of interdisciplinary spokesperson that the field of animal studies needs.

I asked Debbie how humans can use their faculty of intuition to get closer to animals. Debbie responded that there are so many layers to the animal mind that we are not even aware of, and that animals are here to show us their capacities if we will listen, and not allow human limitations to influence our judgment. Debbie explained that animals can sense natural disasters, and that they have a quasi-supernatural ability to sense medical disorders in humans, yet we live in a society that wants to suppress animals not despite but perhaps *because* of these gifts. "Once we recognize all that they are capable of, then we would want to suppress them even more. That is quite terrifying for a lot of people," she explained.

I'm not out to terrify anyone by sharing Brady's

letter. I accept that together, we tapped into this ancient way of expressing ourselves and tuning into one another, and that Brady had much to teach me. I asked Debbie if she thought humans were ready to hear about soulmate dogs, and she said:

Yes. People are hungry to hear what makes humans and dogs so closely bonded to one another. People who have lost animals grieve so deeply, and you can characterize these relationships on a soul level.

Having addressed the issue of a dog that writes letters, I would like to turn to the content of the letter itself. At the time that I received it, I had just come from the delirium of Brady's illness, and the prophetic messages were lost on me. Only now do I understand them. He told me, "We will continue on our path together as I have a second chance at life as I see it." Check. Our Sedona road trip was a second chance at life.

He told me that our purpose was to help others, which I hope we did by co-writing this book, and that "we were to work together in a way that had not been done before." Check: co-authoring a book with a dog. Perhaps that has not been done before after all.

I even consulted with Brady about editing this book, and he has had many surprising suggestions that were detailed and spot on. He kept reminding me that this was about a journey of healing, redemption, and love, and that it was not only his journey but mine, something I had been leaving out. He said, "You see our souls intersect in ways that others do not." The chapter on contending with philosophy affirms that.

Lastly, he said: "You are a fearless warrior for my health, and for that I am grateful." Double check. But when Brady said that this was not only about his journey, but also about mine, perhaps he was alluding to something that hadn't occurred to me yet.

The parallels between our spirochetal diseases

would become uncanny years down the road, as I fought to save my own life (which is another story, for another book). I would remember that he had told me that the (joint) journey was about healing, redemption, and love. The power of love was our primary ingredient that carried us through his dark times with lepto, and it would sustain me through my battle with Lyme. It spread through our community, as others showed their love by helping us. Conversely, by sharing our medical recovery stories with you, I hope that we can help many others. These were the gifts that came from our illnesses. Our upswing, if you will.

Coda

I wanted to write this book to share a nonhuman animal's ability to transcend medical diagnoses and live a long life having overcome obstacles. I wanted it to reveal and revel in the language of Dog. I wanted to show how becoming fluent in that language changed my perspective on nonhuman animals. I did not want this to be like so many other books about dogs, in which the beloved dog died, and the reader sobbed at home, or on an airplane, or in a coffee shop, while reading the pages describing the dog's death. In Chapter 42 of one of my favorite novels, *Genji Monogatari,* or *The Tale of Genji,* written in 1010 by Japanese authoress Murasaki Shikibu, the protagonist Prince Genji dies abruptly on page 788 of 1184 pages. The narrator recounts it so as to startle the reader with no notice: "The shining Genji was dead, and there was no one quite like him."[58] I was so stunned when I first read *Genji* that I flung the heavy book on the floor and cried for a while before I could pick it up and continue reading it.

In Mozart's 41st symphony, the finale consists of a complex fugue—a lengthy coda of sorts—that draws together the themes of the previous movements, while creating new material, unlike the traditional connotation of a coda that functions primarily to recapitulate, to provide a "tail," as the word is meant in Italian. I'm following Mozart's formula here.

On Tuesday, October 25th, 2016, I wrote the following, which I quote in full, unedited:

Brady died in my arms Monday morning, October 24th, 2016, at 3:08 a.m. His body failed fast within a few days to the point that he lost his dignity. On Friday afternoon, our new local doctor in Pound Ridge, New York, said we should help Brady leave his body through medical means since he could no longer walk easily, and he declined food. After five days of IV fluids, Brady's kidney values remained extremely elevated for the first time. Startled and disconsolate, yet eager to alleviate Brady's suffering, we agreed to bring him to Pound Ridge Vet on Monday morning.

D and I made a pact to be strong and joyful for Brady all weekend. We made a makeshift bed in the foyer so that we could carry Brady outside quickly, though we didn't always make it in time. Brady did not appear to be in pain, but he was enervated. He still lifted his head to kiss us when we reached down to him. We never left Brady's side, but we carried his bed on all four corners like a royal litter around the house and outdoors so he could bask in the sunlight, the autumn breeze, and the light of the stars at night.

I had always hoped that when Brady left the world one day, I would be holding him at home. I feared not being with him when he departed. I always wished that his departure would be on his terms. On Sunday night, Brady was very weary, but he still kept his watchful eyes on me at all times. I held his paws, held his gaze, and said softly, "You have my permission to go. I know you will always protect me in spirit, and I want you to be free." I gently repeated these words. Brady and I went to sleep side by side at midnight, his paw in my hand. He woke me up a little later by urgently licking my head, my hair, and my face for a long time. He even put his whole nose in my mouth, a first. He nuzzled my head and neck like a horse. Brady was choreographing a loving farewell for his special girl, I now know. I was cradling him when he shook, heaved violently, shook, and slipped out of the body that could no longer contain his great spirit.

What a gift. Brady chose to die in his own bed at home, not at the hospital where he had spent so much time in the past three years fighting off leptospirosis and chronic renal failure like a warrior. He made sure I was there holding him, and he came to rest in a peaceful sleeping position, curled up in my arms.

Brady will always be my soulmate dog. I loved him as much as anyone ever loved anyone.

I could not stay home and weep in our sanctuary replete with memories and traces. I had to do something radical to grieve the losses of Gram [my beloved mother's mother had fallen and broken her hip at the age of 99] and Brady who died two weeks apart. When D and I brought Brady to be cremated early Monday morning, I wailed out loud and buried my head in his fur one more time before the veterinary technicians carried him away on a stretcher. Then, I picked up my mountaineering backpack, and headed straight for Newark airport, where I took the next flight bound for Buenos Aires. From there, I made my way on planes and long bus rides to Patagonia. I had bursts of accidental weeping as I went. Every flight attendant from New York to El Calafate has hugged me after seeing me clutch photographs of Brady to my chest.

Tomorrow I will embark on an epic solo trek through the isolated Torres del Paine mountain range for ten days to heal. I suspect I will sob, laugh, and brim with the love Gram and Brady bestowed on me. I will shake off my Lyme aches, and learn to begin again. They say there is no cell service in the mountains of Chile, so I shall be off the grid with only the contents of my mountaineering backpack. Along with a tent and a camping stove, for instance, I have my journal and one slim volume of Emerson essays.

To all of you who loved Brady, and he had many dear friends among you, thank you. May we all experience such contentedness with another being at least once in our lives. I am broken, yet grateful to have known such pure love. As Brady's good friend Jim Lowe wrote on Monday, "A dog was never better loved. Hell, a person was never better loved."

As Brady told me in a conversation with Debbie a few weeks prior to his death, "The end is never the end. Love never ends." Brady's book doesn't end with his death.

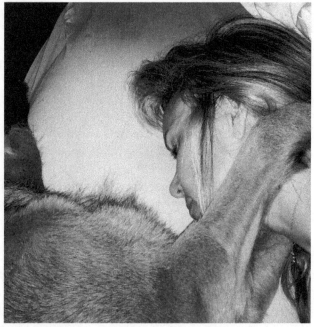

A candid shot of true love.

One needs to grieve the loss of one's soulmate dog. We who have soulmate dogs are pioneers; we are writing a new history. In her foreword to prominent grief experts Elisabeth Kübler-Ross and David Kessler's text *On Grief and Grieving,* Maria Shriver writes that we are "a grief-illiterate nation." [59] If we don't know how to express grief for our humans, we surely don't have the vocabulary to grieve for our companion animals. I consistently wrote in my journal throughout Brady's life, chronicling our lives together, and those entries helped me grieve.

Brady overcame so many health crises that I had begun to think he was invincible after our battle against death in 2013. We had three very high-quality years together after he was released from the emergency hospital, although they were volatile ones. Brady had ups and downs with chronic renal failure, and I was sick with what the doctors were calling chronic Lyme disease. There were many times in the last few years of Brady's life that I could barely walk up and down the stairs at home, but I sacrificed my own health to take care of him. He was my priority; he was my rock.

By the middle of the summer in 2014, I had a resurgence of debilitating Lyme symptoms. Once again, I was shut down, unable to read, to write, or even to drive. Debbie would tell me, "Even though you feel weak, you never stop helping him." Brady was my radiant light in this time; he had fought so hard to stay alive for me that I fought hard to be well for him.

We needed help, though. Friends stayed for days at a time to take care of us and make meals. Brady was so thankful to the friends who were helping us that he would lick them, wag his tail for them, and even go to sleep on some of their beds to keep them company. In our role reversals, Brady had become Head Nurse for Team Miche. Brady would say, "Let's get you to play more." Or he would say, "I'm feeling very protective of you right now. You don't have the strength so I need to watch over you carefully right now."

On days that I was flattened by Lyme, Brady would come over, lick my face thoroughly, and sit down on my feet for a while. He was always my comforter. We can add that to his list of well-played roles.

In the fall of 2016, I thought that I had nearly finished editing this manuscript with a concluding "Where are we today?" section. Just weeks later, I wrote in my journal, "Who did I think we were, Icarus and companion?" Did I really think we could defy the limits of longevity? We did do that, but it could not be done infinitely with Brady in his ailing physical body. Elizabeth Kübler-Ross consoles those who grieve: "We know intellectually that we don't have forever. […] But intellect does not inform matters of the heart."[60]

Brady's final year, 2016, started out auspiciously. We took a robust walk in the Ward reservation in Pound Ridge with D on New Year's morning. There was no snow, but there was a panoply of fallen maple leaves, and it reminded me of how I had longed to hike there with Brady when he was imprisoned by leptospirosis at the hospital.

New Year's Day 2016 hike in Pound Ridge. "Brady, do you have a new year's wish?" "I just take it one day at a time." Photo credit: Dmitri Sinenko

During our winter in Houston, Brady seemed to need a lot of IV fluids, but he was energetic and stable. Given our ability to communicate closely, I was able to help him quickly each time he had a new health issue. I would take him to our caring vet Dr. Christine Orengo at the cozy *Noah's Ark Animal Hospital*, just a short mile from our house. Brady said in March, "Being a good patient comes in handy because I feel better when I get help. I was quite honestly feeling miserable. I have been a lot of work lately. I'm sorry." I replied to him: "It's never work to take care of you. It's always my pleasure."

As we were packing up to return to Connecticut for the summer, I thanked Dr. Orengo for all that she and her staff had done for Brady this past winter. She said: "We will miss Brady this summer. He is just like a human child.

He is so expressive and he has the mannerisms of a child, being quiet all day and then barking when you walk into the reception area. He says, 'Mom! I'm here, don't forget me!'" I had asked them to use the metal basket muzzle on him while they inserted catheters, not knowing how he would react after having had nearly three years of catheters inserted into his veins. Dr. Orengo told me that he would lick them through the muzzle, so they stopped using it.

The summer of 2016 brought another overwhelming medical crisis, and one that could have been averted. Brady had stem cell surgery on July 13th. Dr. Nate thought it would really help Brady, so we were willing to take the risk, but it contributed to Brady's demise.

Veterinarians have been using stem cell therapy from autologous adipose-derived adult stem cells to treat degenerative diseases since 2007; thousands of horses, cats, and dogs have been treated since then. Most canine treatments have focused on arthritic issues, but companies such as Vet Stem are expanding their research on using stem cell therapy for organ disease and failure. Hence, Brady's stem cell therapy was somewhat experimental.

On the appointed day, I signed the consent form for the surgery and noticed that Dr. Nate had inserted the word "between" in the middle of "last" and "resort" as a reason for the stem cell therapy. He was going to extract 40 grams of fat from Brady and ship it medical express to a lab in Kentucky named MediVet Biologics. The lab would process it, create millions of stem cells, and send it back. Dr. Nate would then use an IV to put the cells back into Brady. Ideally, the stem cells would contain regenerative cells that produce inflammation reducing cytokines. MediVet claims that out of 155 canines that it treated with stem cell therapy for severe osteoarthritis, 99 percent of canines showed improvement after 90 days. MediVet states that it has been seeing some "exciting results" for cases of end-stage renal disease, and liver and kidney failure, claiming that it's safe. As Brady's health-care advocate, I was willing to try any procedure that promised exciting results, particularly a treatment deemed safe.

What Dr. Nate didn't tell me is that it was a major surgery. When I saw Brady post-surgery, I thought: *I would never have consented to this.* Brady had been put under anesthesia, and he had been sliced open. There was a long series of heavy-duty staples down his back, far worse than what he underwent in Wisconsin. I was horrified.

The next day, I wrote, "I am the shell of Michelle today. Brady came through his surgery yesterday, yet I was unprepared for the scars, the sutures, the bare-naked rectangle of skin, and industrial staples holding his flesh together. He cried all night, in spite of the pain medications I administered to him. He snuggled up to me with his head moving from my shoulder to my chest as he shifted in pain. We did not sleep much; he got up to scratch at the sutures, and I would stop him. I dragged the mattress onto the floor so that we could be together. No jumping for him with those sutures."

The surgery site quickly developed a seroma, which is swelling from a pocket of serous fluids that develops in the body after surgery. "Nuts," Dr. Nate said in frustration and disbelief when he saw the seroma developing. Because of the seroma, Brady couldn't receive subcutaneous fluids at home for over a month because the injection site was too close to the swelling.

At that point in Brady's life, D and I had adjusted our schedules to give Brady subcutaneous fluids twice a day. D would rush home from work to be my assistant vet tech, and he would wake me up early so we could give Brady our early morning infusion before he went to work. Sometimes he was head vet tech, and had one of his friends assist if I was out at one of my many doctor's appointments. Brady was very good-natured about it. Our friends had become involved, squeezing the bag for us after we inserted the syringes. We were professionals at fluid administration, even stopping to do it on our road trips to and from Houston.

The stem cell surgery was all for naught, because MediVet reported that the quality of Brady's cells was so poor that they could not generate the requisite millions of stem cells that they had hoped for. Instead, Brady had drainage tubes coming out of his infected surgery site, and it drained his vitality. Stem cell therapy, while it may be beneficial to many canines, sounded Brady's death knell.

In mid-August, I had a short trip to France planned to attend an important funeral. Dr. Nate decided to keep Brady at his house overnight while I was gone. I was reassured that my friend was in healing hands, but I also felt tremendous guilt in leaving him. Shockingly, two days before my return home, I received a text from Dr. Nate saying that he thought Brady was in his final days.

I panicked and called Debbie. Debbie couldn't consult with me until 1:00 a.m. local time, so I stayed up and meditated before our call. I had recorded Vijaya's waterfall meditation some years before, and I played it on my phone as I sat cross-legged in bed, eyes closed. I connected with Brady's energy and then I went through a very visual meditation of standing in a waterfall and cleansing my energy. It was very powerful, and it worked to alleviate my anxiety.

When I spoke to Debbie, she said, "I know this isn't right because Brady is at Dr. Nate's house, but he says he has just been swimming!" I told her that he had been swimming during our waterfall meditation. This amazed her. "Miche, he totally perked up when I told him I had you on the phone, but his body is so weak and tired. The toxins are backing up in his body and there is a lot of bile that burns and makes him feel lousy." Debbie paused, and said gently, "Brady is showing me that he is backing out of his body. He is becoming more of a light body because the physical body is demeaning to him now."

I started sobbing quietly, but I kept writing every word down, as I always did. "Miche, he has messages for you: 'As you know, we will be together forever. A few things are shifting out of control. I am becoming ethereal. You are my beautiful healer. You never tire of trying to help me. Your love is effortless.'" I couldn't really speak, so

I just wrote and listened. "He is just so tired. He's having a hard time catching up. He says, 'It doesn't matter where you are; we are always together. You should know this. You're very silly not to know this. Sometimes we are more powerful energetically.'" Debbie realized that I couldn't speak, so she kept reassuring me, "Keep doing what you are doing. The water exercises are grounding."

I asked if Brady had a message for Dr. Nate, and he did: "He is like an uncle to me. I am very comfortable with him. I will not give the good doctor another scare. I am waiting for you." I begged Brady to wait for me, to not die when I was far away in France. Debbie replied, "He is so stubborn and strong. He understands, but says wisely, 'This is not for you to decide, but I am holding on and I will wait for you.'"

I couldn't wait to get home. Dad, Janet, and D picked Brady up from Dr. Nate, and lavished him with attention. Then D drove Brady home to Connecticut just as I would be arriving from the airport. I just plunked down on the grass and he sat down on top of my legs, drainage tubes and all, looking as gaunt as could be. *I won't leave your side.*

August 24, 2016: "Nursing Brady around the clock, but happy to stay with him faithfully. He still has so much joy and life in him. Yesterday I played my saxophone for him. We played outside with the ball and we lay in the sun together, paw in hand. We watched a movie in the movie theatre, which he loved." We made every day a beautiful day at that time; it was *carpe diem* time for us.

When I slowly pulled the drainage tubes out of him, it became a messy, bloody venture beyond my capacities as a veterinary technician. Blood was oozing out of them. Brady had told Debbie that his body was demeaning to him, and I sadly understood why.

I checked in with Debbie shortly thereafter: "His energy feels a lot better to me, Miche. He says he's been having a blast. He's not obsessed about his body. He's just enjoying things. I'm not seeing that vacancy in his eyes. I don't know what his body is going to end up doing, but he is enjoying himself. I see that brightness in his eyes. He's just been having fun. You always worry about quality of life, but he is happy. I don't see that dark, depressed energy; his energy is more consistent." I was administering three liters of subcutaneous fluids a day by now, and I asked Debbie how he was managing with the invasive routine.

"He's very patient with the fluids, Miche. He's gotten accustomed to the process, but he doesn't like it. He just looks at you with these adoring eyes. He has been very happy this past week."

I asked, "Debbie, does he want to go to see Dr. Nate again soon?" I had been driving to Vermont once a week, and then staying in Burlington for 10 hours a day while he got fluids. We were both exhausted by the routine. We were even staying in a hotel to avoid the hour-long commute to Dad's.

Brady made a wise choice, and one that I honored: "Dr. Nate has done an excellent job, but as my body slows down, I want to spend less time in the hospital and more time with my family at home."

I started to break down into tears and I asked awkwardly, "How will I know when it will happen, when he will leave his body?"

"Things are holding steady right now, but you'll know. When the body says it's enough, it will be a rapid decline."

Debbie continued: "You're giving him a miracle. Now he is filled with joy and happiness."

"Debbie, I never wanted to put him down. I wanted him to choose with dignity. What do I do if he is in pain?"

Debbie responded gently. "Some animals are adamant that they pick the time they want to leave. Some animals take too long. Sometimes it is a gift to alleviate the pain. Right now, you are doing the best thing for him. His body was polluted before."

I had one last message for Brady during this poignant conversation. "Debbie, please tell Brady that he is my biggest gift of this lifetime. He is my joy."

She answered, "Miche, he knows. He says, 'We are always together for a reason. The end is never the end.'"

I clung to these words, and I read them over and over again.

I needed to honor Brady's wishes. At the very end of August, I found a vet in Pound Ridge, just two miles from my house on back country roads. We had stopped going to Smith Ridge Vet when Dr. Mike left since they could not administer multiple bags of fluids to Brady through the IV system they used. Pound Ridge Vet had excellent reviews, so we made an appointment. It was a calm, quiet office with an interesting architectural design that backed up to a rocky ledge in the trees. Brady and I really liked Dr. Kaddatz, who resembled a warm and witty grandfather. He was a methodical, almost fastidious man when it came to testing all of the possibilities, just my kind of a doctor. We ran several blood serum tests, and decided that Brady needed serious help. Dr. Kaddatz spoke to me as if I understood all of the medical vocabulary, which I did by that time. I had graduated from Amateur Nephrologist to Expert Nephrologist over the past three years.

We decided that Brady would have IV fluids all day for six days, and that I would pick Brady up in the late afternoon every day. Dr. Kaddatz recommended low-protein canned kidney food and kibble, which looked revolting to me, but I was willing to throw all of my ideals out and try anything. We started this routine, and Brady responded very well.

It was not a sustainable routine, though, for either of us. D had gone to Singapore and I was in charge of the meals, thrice-daily fluids, veterinary shuttle rides, medications, and taking Brady out several times during the night as a result of vast quantities of intravenous and subcutaneous fluids. Dr. Nate sent me a compression pump that I could attach to the bag of fluids. So, without D's assistance, I made my music stand into a makeshift IV stand, and I pumped the fluid bag with my spare hand that wasn't holding the syringe in place. As always, I was a warrior for Brady.

My friend Josh texted one morning, worried that I would break if Brady died. Josh, who is terribly allergic to dogs, loved Brady. I texted back: "I am sleep deprived and weary, that is true, but I rest when Brady sleeps. I know that no human can truly fathom this bond that Brady and I have, but I am humming with joy when I am with him, and I feel like our beings are intertwined in spirit when we are together." I continued, "I have never felt this before with anyone. I know how peculiar it sounds." Josh responded, "No, I understand completely. It's not hard to imagine. It's just rare."

We had the gift of an Indian summer—the season paralleled our time together, for we had many good days in September and October. It was as if we were given lost time back from 2013, and we capitalized on every autumnal day.

I wondered if Brady would be up for his favorite activity. I wondered if that would be on his bucket list. We padded out to the pool every day and swam our synchronized laps together. When I glanced over at him, I would say, "Are we going to the doggie Olympics this year?" D cheered for us as he videotaped us. He had come back abruptly from Singapore for "personal reasons" when he realized how dire our circumstances were at home. D snapped many photos of us swimming with oak leaves falling into the pool that symbolized our Indian summer, and then he surprised me that Christmas with a framed photo of me and my soulmate dog swimming that fall.

Synchronized swimmers attached at the hip. The summer of 2016.
Photo credit: Dmitri Sinenko

My journal entry from September 4, 2016, sums up the atmosphere of this time:

"We are both humming with a quiet joy this morning. Waking was *achey* and painful for both of us, I expect. Brady followed me around the garden, played with his ball, and looked very happy."

On September 15th, I celebrated Brady's marker. "It has been three years since Brady went into the emergency hospital. I am so grateful for those three years that we have had together. My miracle dog."

Then, we both had an unexpected surge of vitality. We took little walks by the stream on the bike path, pausing to let Brady enjoy the breeze from the running water. We curled up in the rose garden together. When I grew fearful, an image came to me of a pressure cooker valve opening. It let the stress and fears burst out at once. It was working.

Brady was voracious at this time and he was eating large meals every day with no coaxing. Dr. Kaddatz said: "Brady is beyond amazing." Dr. Nate texted me: "Brady is a tank." Debbie said: "He is a very advanced soul, Miche."

On September 24th, I had my penultimate conversation with Debbie and Brady, and it took place during our burst of vitality. Debbie connected with Brady for a long time quietly, and then she said, "It's like he was infused with this young vitality. He speaks to me with a young voice. He is pushing through all of this with supernatural force. He is overriding his body, Miche." Debbie said, "He showed me the music that you are playing for him, which he loves. He says the music is healing you, too. He is laughing at everything you do to make each day special. He thinks it's funny and he appreciates it."

Brady showed me that music is — what Longfellow called — a universal language for humans and nonhuman animals. He had a very strong affinity for music, and he watched me intently when I played. Playing music for Brady was one of the gifts that I could give him.

I had one last question. "Is the writing affecting him?" "Miche, he loves when you write. He says, 'I just choose to be away from it if you are writing about the emergency hospital.'" When I worked on the chapters that narrated Brady's experience in the hospital, Brady would head out of the library. "Debbie, I feel like he has been helping me with my writing." "Yes, Brady said 'sometimes I put on my professor cap. I have been pushing her to write. That's been fun for me.'"

Brady's last good photo. In the autumn of Brady's life, in Vermont.

I had been invited to an alumni event at my old boarding school, and Brady would be staying with my dad and Janet and being treated by Dr. Nate one last time. On October 5th, when we were in Vermont, Debbie and I had our last conversation with Brady after I thought Brady had a mini-stroke. He had been shaking and expelled his bladder. Then he fell down the stairs in Connecticut before we came up to Vermont. Debbie reported: "Miche, he's still feeling weak to me, and it could be the anemia, but he's happy to be in Vermont. I'm getting a drained feeling from him, though, and also a craving for beef and liver. He is admitting he felt disheveled and confused, so maybe he was having a mini-stroke. I'm getting that before the fall, maybe it was a seizure. He's trying to show me something else here. He is still not fully grounded in his body. He wants to be ungrounded in his body. Being out of his body he is smiling. He is half out. You can attempt to do some re-grounding."

Debbie continued, sharing Brady's comments: "However, he doesn't like being in his body anymore, because it feels so weak, so he would rather be out of it."

I told Debbie that I had a stressful encounter just before Brady's energy plummeted, and it had sapped my own vitality. Brady said: "We certainly ride on each other's energy. The vibe has been strong. It has been lovely. Now, it is slow and heavy like we got energetically punched. What happens to you travels to me and vice versa."

Debbie said, "I will tell him he mustn't take on those emotional things that humans go through. But he said, 'It's not her fault. I choose to be plugged into her.'" Brady had several more messages for me in a row:

"If this is my last lesson here, you are loved for yourself, for who you are. I fear that you lose this sometimes."

It broke me to hear those words.

"I see you sometimes. You walk with an upbeat energy, but you walk with a heavy heart. I don't want you to let my illness bring you down. My illness is a transformation of sorts.

"Your life has more value than you give it credit for. Some people prepare for emergencies like hurricanes, but you need to prepare for emotionally hurtful things that hurt deeper. When things get ugly, you must get strong."

He had me figured, and he exposed all of my vulnerable spots.

"He does say it would be good for you to go away to Interlochen this weekend, as planned, for the meetings. You need a change of energy and a change of scenery. It's vital for you to get out of this pattern of energy right now.

"Also, please tell the good doctor not to panic when he sees my numbers."

I was crying again by this time, because I knew that the end was coming soon. Brady felt this, and here is what he told Debbie in his final conversation with us:

"My energy and my being and my soul are bigger than me. I have more to do with you in your life. You must know that we have made a contract for eternity. Don't be fooled by this weak body that I have; it's just a piece of paper. I'm not trying to scare you, but whenever I decide to leave, it will be my decision."

I was sobbing so audibly that Debbie said: "He has a very strong will and he will wait for you to return from Interlochen."

Debbie interrupted Brady's flow to say: "He sees all of these great things for you, on a big level, beyond the individual. Old ways, old habits falling aside, rebirthing fresh. A new energy will come. There is so much more for you. He's excited for you and very proud. You mustn't feel guilty. Do not suppress yourself. Your knowledge is intimidating. The boat is springing a leak. The leak is your unworthiness. You are a fighter and you just need to believe in yourself. 'These are great quotes, and she should be writing them down!'" Brady always did have a sense of humor, but he was right, and I did write them down, in my stupor.

Then, we entered the last few words of Brady's conversation, and he became even more serious. Debbie said, "He says to me that when he leaves this lifetime, he will come back to you in this lifetime, in this species: 'I will come back when she has fixed her problem of self-worth. It will be a different time and place. I need to give her a challenge. She's competitive, you know.'"

I laughed and cried simultaneously at this, but I was also shell-shocked.

Brady left me with words to repeat, "I'm greater than my human capacity." Debbie said, "Know that he wants you to go to Interlochen. Be the best you can. This is very important."

The last conversation was so monumental that I have had to read it and process it many times. If I put pressure on the reader to overcome skepticism about telepathic communication with animals, now I would be putting even more pressure on the reader to believe in animals as prophetic messengers, or even as psychologists. At best, even I had to take wild liberties with acknowledgement, my favorite philosopher Cavell's offering of what he calls a "mode of feeling to replace knowing" as a solution to the potential impasse implicit in skepticism when it comes to claiming to know the thing in itself.[61]

Regarding Brady's messages: I do not find vulnerability enchanting. I strive to show my strength to the world instead. Brady's comments show just how vulnerable I really am, just how the mainstream philosophers describe the animals. I thought about editing them out, for of course there is much that I have left out. This is not an autobiography, but when Brady told me that this book is about my journey, too, I believe this is what he meant. My worry about being worthy—as a writer, a musician, an academic—had resided in me for years, in spite of my hard work. I would contemplate his words for a long time.

I did go to Interlochen for two days, and just as Brady indicated, it was important. I was invited to give lectures in the winter on the intersection between climate change and the arts, a subject dear to me. When I was at Interlochen, Brady's numbers went haywire again, and he was vomiting bile at Dad and Janet's. When we went back home, Brady spent Monday through Friday with Dr. Kaddatz getting IV fluids.

Something terrible happened for the first time, and

that was my clue: Brady's creatinine jumped up from 5.7 to 7.7 at the end of five days. That 7.5 was an all-time high. By Wednesday, he could barely walk any longer. By Friday, Dr. Kaddatz said Brady was failing, and that we should spend a last weekend with him, and then help him out of his body on Monday morning.

I was sitting on my purple velvet meditation chair when I had the phone conversation with Dr. Kaddatz. It was the same chair I sat on to meditate through Brady's acute crisis, manifesting his recovery day after day, doggedly. This time, I thought I would faint right off the chair. I called my dad.

"I can't believe it," Dad wailed. "It can't be true!" I cried with him. "We've come so far," he whimpered. We were grieving together in advance. Though I didn't realize it at the time, this was a groundbreaking opportunity for Dad and me to be present with the dreaded experience of shock over losing our shared loved one. We would cry together many times. Dad had loved Brady as I had, and this time, we *acknowledged our shared pain.* It's as if sharing our pain with one another healed the faint scars from when my mother died and neither one of us knew how to grieve, how to share. We had both been lonely in our grief about mom and Joy, but this time, we would mourn together, hand in hand. (Still, Dad had his limits. Although Dad read everything I had ever written, when I sent him an early draft of this book, he couldn't open it. "It's just too sad for me," he confessed.)

Then, I called D. I told D that we would have a celebration of Brady that weekend. "We'll do whatever you need," he said.

I wanted Brady to retain his dignity, but it was a 24-hours-a-day challenge for everyone, but mostly for him. We just loved him and cleaned him and helped him, and he licked us and snuggled and expressed that he simply wanted to be with us. We moved our mattress downstairs into the foyer so we could take him out quickly. He kept his eyes on me all of the time.

187

On his last night, he did not want me to leave his side. I would walk around to put things away and he looked for me. I was not to leave; it was clear. Then it happened the way I wrote that it did.

The most important thing to me in Brady's death was that he chose his place and time as a way of demonstrating his dignity, his agency in the face of a failing physical body. And I recognized the value in that dignity as another way of acknowledging his worth as a fellow being. Recalling Derrida's argument that finitude and mourning are inextricably related, privileging Brady's dignity in death is to say that his finitude was worth something important, and that he was worthy of being loved, being mourned.

The trek in Patagonia was my homage to Brady. I know he was with me. At first all of the travel distracted me from the devastation of Brady's loss. I would like to include some of my raw and random journal entries in this section; they are not polished. Grief is not polished. I believe that grieving Brady was also an integral part of this journey that the two of us had been on for nine years. I concur with grief experts David Kessler and Elizabeth Kübler-Ross on the importance of grieving: "If you do not take the time to grieve, you cannot find a future in which loss is remembered and honored without pain."[62]

October 25, 2016
It is quite the trek to reach Torres del Paine, or the blue towers. Thus far, I flew from Connecticut to Houston, Houston to Buenos Aires, missed my next flight, took a taxi to another airport to change flights, and now I am on a five-hour plane ride south to El Calafate, deep in the land of Patagonia. The travel is distracting me from my grief for Brady, but I think of him constantly. I keep thinking how extraordinary it is that Brady choreographed his death in the most beautiful way. It was his final act, his coda, his final bars. They will resonate with me always. I knew a

perfect love. I had that great gift.[63]

Before I lost all cell service in the Andes, I received the following text messages:

10/24 6:48 a.m. "Free dog...may our precious Jolly Ball dog rest in peace. Much loved Brady will live on in our hearts and memories forever and be enormously missed. Blessed are we to have had him in our lives." — Janet

7:41 a.m. "It is heartbreaking. The children and I all cried for Brady at breakfast." — Helen

9:42 a.m. "I am so glad he was in your arms. I think the fact that he went on his own terms is beautiful. You have been the best mommy in the world to him. I still remember meeting you when you arrived home from Wisconsin and you were upset that he had lost one of his Gore-Tex booties and he could get road salt in his paws on our walk. And boy did he protect you! How precious that he kept kissing you and in his own way he was comforting you. I love you, Miche." — Paula

17:49 p.m. "Oh, Miche. How wonderful that he left his body, while in your arms, what a gift. Sending you big hugs. And he is running and jumping and twirling...by the water...looking for sticks. He is free. — Debbie

23:19 p.m. "I just received this message right now. I'm so very sorry, and a little stunned, even though I knew he was fading. What an incredible creature, and a teacher for me. I'll never, ever forget him. I will finish my reflections about treating him tonight and send them along. I'm very sorry for you and D. I know that bond between you and Brady is very, very deep. How wonderful to travel in physical space with him for nine years. And at some point spirits are meant to be reunited. I know you'll grieve deeply. Remember that Brady could always sense your physical presence without your physical presence, so this will continue. You cared so amazingly well for him. Thank you for letting us be a part of it. Sincerely, Nate"

These messages were very meaningful for me, and I carried them with me as I prepared to hike.

October 27

Bus from El Calafate to Puerto Natales. I feel like a real adventurer. I am now traversing kilometers of rugged Wyoming-like spaces. Guanacos run across the road. Shaggy sheep roam. I see white peaks ahead in the far distance.

In Puerto Natales this morning, the sight of dogs made me cry. It was the first time I had really seen dogs since Brady died. I see the words, "Brady died," and I start weeping again.

October 27

I am solo. On the bus to Laguna Amarga, my penultimate form of transportation to Torres del Paine. Next comes the catamaran. Last night I posted the eulogy that I wrote on the plane and in the bus on Facebook and on Instagram. I saw the first few comments before I lost cell service permanently for the duration of the hike. People loved Brady. They thought he was majestic. He had so many friends. Friends even came to say goodbye to him, traveling up on the train from Brooklyn.

October 27

Every time I think about Brady I whimper. I do it out loud without thinking. All of the signs here say "no pets allowed" and I get that German shepherds and pumas don't mix, but Brady would love hiking here. Besides, he was not a pet. "Pet" sounds so condescending, and it couldn't begin to account for him.

The jags and crags of the Andes are on an immense scale. When I got out of the bus to register in the park, I was knocked over twice by the wind, backpack and all. The wind sent me flying into a bush. I hope that it is not an omen.

Brady will be with me. I will not forget what Dr. Nate wrote to me in his text: "Remember that Brady could always sense your physical presence, so this will continue."

October 29

At Erratic Rock, the makeshift basecamp in Puerto Natales that held daily lectures on climbing Torres del Paine, they told us that we would see all four seasons in one day on the trail: sun, still, rain, wind, and frigidity. My emotions are like the Patagonian weather. I am fragmented, yet I am finding strength as I hike.

I am sporadically weeping in my tent, dressed in layers of wool and down. I'm sitting cross-legged, eating my dinner. I make whimpering sounds involuntarily, startling myself.

My boy.

There is already a crater in my heart. I feel him shimmering and leaping in the woods next to me as I hike. He is free. I am free. It is revolutionary. But when I remember that his physical presence is gone, I feel the crater cracking open in my chest.

Yesterday I planned to do a civilized seven-and-a-half-kilometer hike to Campamento Italiano, and call it a day. Yet the Brazilian solo hiker I met at basecamp, Fabiano, and his fellow Brazilian hiker, Fabio, would not let me trek alone. I felt like Brady was protecting me in spirit.

Once we reached Campamento Italiano, by way of a hair-raising suspension bridge, it was only 11:30, and I felt a rush of accomplishment at making it through a first leg. Fabio and Fabiano were raring to start their Valles Frances hike, which was an additional 12 km. The idea was to drop the heavy packs at Italiano, do the roundtrip, and carry on for three kilometers to Camping Frances for the night. It was only 11:30 and I was planning to camp at Italiano. I felt fairly good, though, which amazed me, and the Brazilian hikers were arguing, "You can't stay in this rundown camp with one festering portable potty."

The terrain was surprisingly varied. First, we met with gravelly gray rocks, then we were underneath green forests passing water falls, drinking straight from them. There were glaciers to the left, waterfalls in the mountains, and craggy rocks to behold. Finally, after six kilometers of intense hiking, we were on top of the rock at Mirador Brittanico, or British lookout.

The mountains were god-like. I was not expecting that. There was a panorama of spectacular mountains in full sunshine. We frolicked on top of a flat rock, taking photographs. It felt therapeutic.

We trekked down to Campomento Italiano, and I looked at my health app on the iPhone, which I could charge with my portable battery packs. We had done 12 miles for the day. I was incredulous. I do not have the capacity to hike 12 miles. I have an aching, spirochete-ridden body that limits me most of the time. *What is happening to me? Is the adrenalin of grief fueling me?*

Fabio and Fabiano convinced me to go to Camping Frances with them, for Frances was brand new and had solar showers. I groused, but I went with them. There were wooden platforms at Frances, for the hillside was too steep to pitch tents. We were given a box of nails and a hammer to secure our tents to the platform. Fabiano helped me nail down my tent. I wondered if Brady had sent Fabiano to help me. If he could orchestrate his own death, he could surely orchestrate a little extra help for me in Patagonia.

The next morning we left at 8:30 and I didn't really know what the distances would be, but we hiked 12.1 miles the first day, and by the end of the day, I had hiked 11.8 miles. I did not feel like a mountain goat the second day. I felt like an old, ailing packhorse. It was mostly uphill for 12 miles, and my pack seemed to be getting heavier.

We saw Caribbean-colored glacial waters on the right, extending out for miles and miles. On the left, we saw white-capped, ominous stone outcroppings jutting into the sky. I was with Fabiano and Fabio for the first nine miles, and then we split to stay at two different camping areas. I was to ascend the Chileno pass and stay at Refugio Chileno. I would be halfway up the mountain already for the Torres del Paine sunrise hike, the signature hike of the park.

I have the heaviest backpack of anyone here. I felt — when I left them and I could think — that the heavy load is the symbol for my life. Heavy. Worrying about Brady's health and my own health for the past several years.

I hiked through terrain that resembled Scotland as the landscape abruptly shifted from uphill and downhill stone and gravel to gentle dirt and heather with a mist. There was no passport control to enter "Scotland," just a turn in the trail that led me across a stream, up a hill, and down into a valley of heather.

I turned left onto the Chileno pass trail. Without warning, there were violent hurricane-force winds, and I was careening up a steep pass with a river below. Any false step, and I would have dropped off the trail and into the ravine. The pack was so heavy that the ribbon of a trail in front of me was very daunting. At last, I descended the pass, and on the other side of the river there was a gleaming green roof. Refugio Chileno at long last. I crossed the lovely wooden bridge over the river, and I had arrived. Twenty-six miles in two days in a body that is not in shape for that.

I am happy to be here.

I am Brady's love. He is my love.

He is free.

I am free.

[Though I didn't write it in my journal, it was a lovely campsite, right by the river, high up in the mountains, and very cold. It was full of lively day hikers coming up and down from the Torres hike, and there was a roaring fire by the *refugio* cabin so that the refuge-seekers could have full room and board by the fire. I was more than glad to take my boiling water from the kitchen (no cooking allowed outside here because of the wind), my coffee mug of Chilean wine that I purchased in the cantina, and retreat to my tent. There I could think about Brady, look at his photos, rearrange my "home," and write about the thoughts and events of the day. In a small triumph, I easily set up my tent all by myself. The independent New England girl Brady knew so well is back. In my pack that night, I found a card I had purchased for myself, which read "Difficult journeys lead to beautiful destinations." Indeed.]

I'm curling up in my sleeping bag with my beloved Emerson now.

October 30

Most of the time in Patagonia, I am in such survival mode that I cannot actively mourn for Brady. I am walking out the grief. Each step I take is in honor of him and our bond. It's an Emersonian commitment, a precept of self-reliance that leads me to shed off past selves and walk towards the future. Not arriving at some future perfect self, but moving towards it...This morning, I woke up at 3:30 a.m. when the alarm went off for the Torres del Paine hike. In Patagonia, one cannot see the stars at night. There is profound darkness at night. It was below freezing when I woke, because my nostrils stuck together. It was -9, they said later. I had been advised at Erratic Rock not to hike alone, that hiking in the dark is forbidden because of increased danger of puma attacks, and because of the increased risk of getting lost.

However, the Torres sunrise hike is the quintessential Torres del Paine hike, and to do it, one must start hiking at 3:45 a.m. from Chileno. I had hoped to meet up with another group of hikers, but the shining headlamps told me that I was just behind one group of four, and another group of four literally marched past me as if they were hiking to the inexorable beat of a metronome; I couldn't have kept up.

A large jackrabbit jumped onto the trail in front of me, and I was sure it was a puma. I did lose the trail one time, and it unnerved me, but I located it once again, just before a shaky suspension bridge over a thundering mountain river. Then the wind roared brutally, just as I came to the steep, exposed boulder field. I climbed it, sweating, stripping down to my base layer, worrying that I would be blown off the mountain.

At 5:45 a.m., I reached the top. I crouched behind a sharp, lopsided boulder that was sitting on other precarious boulders. I struggled to put all of my layers back on. The wind bit my face. I had been counseled to bring my sleeping bag to face the cold winds, but it almost blew away along with my backpack. I was clutching all of these items while I gazed out at the horizon.

The sun rose in otherworldly shades of raspberry that started to hit the towers. The towers were tall, narrow spires of flattened rock. They were forbidding. I was surprised to see the outlines of a glacial lake. I could hear the voices of French, German, and British hikers spread out behind various rocks. I was the first one to leave. I thought: *This place is not meant for humans.*

The descent, once I passed the windy boulder field, revealed splendid scenery that my headlamp did not pick up in the dark ascent. I saw the forests, the unique waterfalls, and I just breathed sighs of relief, Brady style. As I descended the boulder field, I encountered an older American couple who were just about to miss the sunrise. The gentleman stopped and said, "This is hard, but it's not insane." But while I was on that hike, I thought, *What am I doing here? This is not safe!* When I finally came to my tent at Chileno, by the bubbling river, on the flattened-out top of a little hillside, with other hikers walking around, I was so relieved.

I had breakfast at the *refugio* that day, which consisted of cold scrambled eggs and hot coffee by the fire. I chatted with a young French couple who had given up their lives in Paris for a year and were hiking South America. I told them that I had come to grieve my dog, and they nodded in sympathy.

Since I only had an 8- to 10-kilometer descent to Camping Torres that day, I took the luxury of slowly breaking down camp and heading down the dreadful pass. On the way down, inching my way with the burdensome pack on my back, I encountered dangerous winds once again on a high narrow pass that made me rethink the remainder of my trip.

I had to stop, brace myself, and then three robust Chilean hikers grabbed me on the narrow pass and had me walk between them. I thought that Brady had sent them to protect me. The wind was fierce, enough to blow anyone over, to knock off hats and sunglasses and make conversation impossible. We crossed the pass and stopped at a steep, gravelly trailhead. The path below looked interminable. I thanked them. I could barely move with my heavy pack. It made the descent very slow going, and I couldn't even aim my foot in the direction where I wanted it to go, and have it land there.

The descent was sunny, but windy. There was a nice hotel in the midst of the park, and it was suddenly very appealing to me. I vacillated between ending my hike altogether, and continuing, but staying at the Hotel Torres tonight. I was already two days early for my next site reservation, much to my surprise. All of my clothes were sweaty, and I hadn't had a proper shower in days. In the past, I would have thought that staying at a nice hotel in the middle of a backpacker's trek was cheating. Who am I cheating, though? This is me choosing my own adventure. And we can always choose our own adventure, I consoled myself.

I chose to stay at the Torres, regroup, and trek on. I took a lukewarm shower, had my laundry done, and made a brilliant decision. I took out about eight kilos of my pack to have sent to Hotel Grey where I would land in about six days. I pulled out extra bags of trail mix, extra clothing, hiking toilet paper and wet wipes. Most importantly, I unloaded my second pair of extremely heavy hiking boots. Who brings two pairs of hiking boots? I was far too experienced a hiker to have made such a neophyte's error, but I had packed in extenuating circumstances.

While I was regrouping, I got a deep-tissue massage. I felt Brady shimmer next to me in approval. Perhaps I am imagining it.

The concierge helped me try to book passage on the Glacier Grey II to exit the park, and he showed me the weather report for Thursday when I would cross the formidable John Garner pass. It is supposed to be cold with 95 km per hour winds. I am scared. I will cross it with Fabiano if I come across him again, and hopefully we will live. I am very tired. I feel like I'm doing all of this in a stupor. My boy died a week ago, now, and I have traveled across the world to grieve him.

October 31

Day One of the back circuit. Now there would be fewer hikers, and only serious ones. Today was the first day that I haven't seen one person on the trail. It was my kind of terrain. It looked like Vermont on a spring day. When I looked up, it looked like Switzerland, but the ground was Vermont.

I read this morning in the hotel museum that the native Patagonians loved dogs. They kept them as companions, warnings, and protection, according to the plaque. So, I'm in the land of the dogs. And my shining one, I know he is with me.

October 31

Brady told Debbie that his illness was a transformation of sorts, and that it had consumed me, and that wasn't right, that the balance was off. I knew that it had consumed me. Here I am, solo, letting the wind sweep the stagnation out of my body, letting it take up all of this sadness, and grief, and loss and channel it into a purposeful new beginning.

Taking those eight kilos out of my pack is symbolic — I was carrying around a pack full of sadness.

November 1

As I was hiking through severe Patagonian wind again today, I thought, the Patagonian exterior weather is a symbol of my internal thoughts. I'm always carrying a heavy load. I also worry that I'm displacing my sadness about Brady. How will I go on living day to day without him? The answer: I won't, because he is with me in spirit. The process of grieving is messy; it does not come in nicely contained packages with well-defined stages.

November 2

I had the gift of hiking by myself this morning, which was cathartic once again. Correction: I was not really alone, because I could feel Brady next to me, shimmering. I know I am repeating this word, but he is truly shimmering, and there is no other way to describe it in English. I left camp just as raspberry and peach ribbons lit up the campsite and illuminated variegated tents pitched on the clearing.

It was dawn's first light when I slung my lighter pack around my back and trotted out of the clearing, following the arrow to Los Perros. I thought of Victor Hugo's poem, which he wrote following the death of his daughter, "Demain, à l'aube, à l'heure où blanchit la campagne, je partirai." *Tomorrow, at dawn, at the hour that whitens the countryside, I will depart.*

As I rose out of the moss-covered forest into alpine terrain with tufts of alpine bushes, rocky outcroppings, and lichen, I turned around and saw a rainbow over Lago Dickson, just as I was crying about Brady. Brady and I had walked in the shadow of a rainbow, just like Gregory Tah-Kloma and Náhani had.

It was Brady's morning gift to me. I looked up and saw yet another set of jagged mountains in a panorama around me. I really took my time this morning, knowing it was one of my last in the park. The terrain was welcoming and comforting. It was just the kind of hike that Brady would have liked.

The sign at Dickson camp indicated that the hike to Los Perros was 8.5 kilometers, but my topographical map measured it at 11.2. Since it was the beginning of the O circuit season on November 1st, there would be almost no hikers coming in my direction, for the trail had just been opened. I had this section of Torres del Paine all to myself. I sat on some logs to drink freshly gathered water from the stream and eat a trail bar. I passed through the protection of many forests with deciduous trees. I listened to songbirds and woodpeckers and crossed rough-hewn bridges that stood in place over bubbling brooks and roaring rivers.

Perhaps my favorite wonder about hiking in Patagonia is that I can fill my water bottle directly from the rivers. It is some of the purest water in the world. I feel like an old American Indian, cupping my hands and drinking out of the stream. My mom and I used to drink water from streams in Vermont. Yet, today, we have polluted everything so much that we have lost this gift of pure mountain water, sadly.

As I continued hiking, I thought again, *How will I live without Brady?* Then, I remembered once again that he had been suffering. When he started running away from me at Dad's and Janet's in mid-October as I approached with my music stand that I suspended the fluid bag from, I was heartbroken. I did not want to hurt my Brady.

When I feel sad, I think that Brady is free. He is a free dog, free from his ailing body that made him feel "disheveled," as he had told Debbie. I have no regrets with Brady. I was grateful for every minute that we had together, and I told him that. I know it was not sustainable for either of us.

November 4

Wednesday was sunny and dry. It would have been the perfect day to cross the infamous John Gardner Pass. In fact, if it had not been for the cruel, petty, bureaucratically driven ranger at Dickson, Fabiano and I would have been crossing the Gardner Pass on Wednesday morning in the sunlight, with no rain or snow.

Fabiano and I had met up again at Séron, and after a beautiful flowing trek of 19 kilometers on Tuesday, we arrived at Dickson, set on a clearing by a glacial beach, surrounded by rocky peaked mountains. It was only 10:45 a.m. It had been our intention to hike to Los Perros from Seron, because we had been forewarned that the weather on the pass would be forbidding on Thursday. If it had not been for the draconian ranger at the Dickson *refugio*, we would not have had to wait to cross it. My reservation at that *refugio* was for November 2 but we arrived on the first.

The ranger with a long black ponytail, a black North Face down jacket, and flashing authoritative eyes told us that we could not leave because his government in Santiago made the rule that everyone had to respect their reservation dates, and that they were cracking down. I said to him, "Respect my safety. I want to be safe." He said, "Respect your itinerary." I said, "What's more important, my itinerary or Mother Nature's variables? I want to be safe." He said, "Follow my rules or I will throw you out of the park." So, reluctantly, Fabiano set up our tents there at Dickson, wasting a good weather day, and squandering the chance to cross the Gardner Pass before 95 km winds and snow set in.

This is the offing for our passage over the John Gardner, where people had died. Rules stated that no one was allowed to cross the pass alone. On Wednesday afternoon, I arrived first at camp Los Perros, at 9:30 a.m. I later found out that 'Perros' means dogs. How appropriate. I chose a campsite the farthest away from the others, so I could easily get on the trail in the morning, and also be away from the hikers who stayed up late chatting and laughing. I rolled back the fly of my tent, since it was so sunny, and I took a long nap. When I woke at noon, I heard the sound of Portuguese. Fabiano and I had met another Brazilian hiker named Gabriel at Dickson, and the two of them must have hiked together from Dickson to Perros.

I took out my dry bags where I stored my food, cooking stove, and journals, and I left my tent to go sit inside the rudimentary building that houses picnic tables and a wood stove. Hikers can safely cook their meals on their camping stoves there, sheltered from the wind. Eileen and David, the older American couple who I had encountered on Torres a few days earlier, eventually arrived. I discovered at Seron that David was a NASA physicist and Eileen was his Caltech biologist wife. We all chatted as it started to rain heavily. It was so cozy there that I stayed through the evening to make my dinner of Cuban black beans and rice, and I did a lot of journal writing. It became crowded and gay, with a lot of backpackers anticipating the passage.

I remembered very late in the day that I had rolled open my fly, and that everything in my tent would be wet. I rushed back in the heavy rain to close my tent fly, but my backpack and sleeping bag were already partially wet. I was so complacent because it hadn't rained for the duration of our trip. It was terribly careless of me.

I tried to lay everything out so it would dry. I packed as best as I could that night so that I could rise the next morning at 4:45 to break down camp for an early morning start to a 22-kilometer day. I slept fitfully.

I had a dream that my grandmother was still alive. She told me that she loved me very much. I was about to call my cousin Anna and tell her that it was all a mistake. When I woke, I realized that Grandma had died, and I felt very disoriented. *What did it mean? Had she come to visit me in a dream? Was she visiting to give me strength for the John Gardner hike?* I didn't know.

It was cold and things were wet in my tent. It was very dark, and for the first time since the gentle morning rain at Paine del Grande on the initial day, it was raining heavily. The dampness brought back the Lyme aches in my hand joints so I struggled to dress.

I chose to wear my warm Smartwool base layers on top and bottom. I donned some black waterproof pants I had grabbed from the closet, my heaviest Smartwool socks, my Patagonia hiking shoes that do not come up over my ankles, and then I decided to put a second base layer on top just in case. Over that, I wore my Arcteryx Gore-Tex coat, which is light, but effective in keeping water out. I wore my fleece-lined wool hat, and my wool neck gaiter. I stuffed my fleece gloves into my pocket for later.

With my headlamp on, I broke down camp and

rushed my backpack over to the shelter. Fabiano was already there, and he had made a fire. "Good morning, Michelle!" "You are never this fast to break down camp," I teased him. "I have been up since 2:00 fretting about the passage," he said. He was raring to go.

I hurried to make my maple raisin oatmeal, the last oatmeal of the trip, thankfully — one and a half packets for more fuel — and made a quick coffee from my Starbucks instant dark roast packets. We were ready to depart at 6:00 a.m. sharp. When I looked down in the cooking room, I realized that the pants I was wearing did not belong to me. Did they belong to D? They hung on me, in the crotch, at the bottom of my legs, and even when I pulled hard on the drawstring, they didn't come close to cinching. I showed them to Fabiano and he laughed. I had to wear them, though, because they were my only waterproof pants, and I had been saving them for a rainy day.

We took off together, no need for headlamps as we were coming into first light, which was quite dark in the presence of the pounding rain. The trail was immediately challenging, and the persistent overnight rain created rivulets as we climbed. We knew we would climb from 565 meters to 1200 meters at the summit of the Gardner pass. The stream crossings became more dramatic, and very soon, water and mud had soaked through my boots and socks, creating my own personal bogs with each step I took. I realized that these unclaimed pants were not waterproof in the slightest, so now I had heavy, low-slinging water traps on my legs. My legs were soaked through my wool base layer so that my skin was drenched. This did not bode well in the mountaineering world.

We continued to climb, and sticky snow started falling on us. Gabriel from Brazil caught up with us. We were three. We were to see no one else for a long time. We climbed out of tree cover onto a steep boulder field. It was impossible to see the trail because of the snow. The wind was furious.

I had to walk in the gargantuan snowy footprints of Fabiano. I took the rear, as my feet and legs were becoming numb and slow. It was a slow trudge, and as we climbed, it was harder to find the orange trail markers. Sometimes we came to a full stop to identify them up ahead. Gabriel and Fabiano took turns trudging ahead to find them, and we zigzagged like Orion's constellation to stay on the trail. Fabiano sunk up to his knees in the snow, and I to my thighs. I could no longer feel my feet and legs, and all I could think of was my father.

D would have been okay without me, but my father would have collapsed if I had died in Patagonia. I had promised him that I would be safe, and I was most assuredly not safe. Dad could not handle losing Brady and me in short succession.

I had taken wilderness survival skills classes in Colorado when I was a summer mountaineering guide there, and I knew what the beginning signs of hypothermia were: mental confusion, numbness, and dehydration. I felt all of these. My feet and legs were frozen. I could not control them, to be precise. I thrust each numb leg out and hoped my foot would land in the right place. My inner voice was stern, "You are to keep moving, and you know it."

After an eon, Gabriel called out, "I see blue sky." I looked high above me and thought that somewhere beyond these killer winds, there was a patch of blue sky. Was I in delirium? The sky tilted oddly.

Then I knew we were in the zenith of the John Gardner "Paso," because the wind was pushing and pulling me viciously, the snow was skimming across a rock surface, and I was seeing an otherworldly, massive, translucent blue glacier down below on the other side. We all hooted and hollered and persevered.

My condition worsened. By the time we started to descend, I was shivering, shaking, mumbling, and had lost control of my limbs and feet. Fabiano said later that it was 10:00 when we started to descend. I remember that. We had been steadily climbing for four hours.

I was so frightened by my symptoms that I started to cry. Once we were in the safety of the trees, Fabiano and

Gabriel sat me down on a tree stump. I could hear them whispering, "She's blue."

Later, they told me they had been terrified. They took off my backpack, pulled off my coat and yanked the top base layer over my head, pulled off the heavy wet pants, and rummaged through my backpack for options. They took off my shoes and put dry socks on. They put my down coat on me, and found a trail bar for me, and put my normal hiking pants on me. Then they fastened my shoes, and we had to keep moving because it was so cold. I didn't remember any of this.

At 11:30, we reached the rudimentary Paso, which consisted of a rickety lean-to. It had been another arduous leg, steep, with snow covering the trail. Paso was cold and desolate, and there was no one there. We took off our shoes and socks and, at the wooden table inside the shelter, Gabriel unearthed his stove, and we boiled water to make a Katmandu vegetable curry from my last dehydrated meal. I had never stopped to make a hot lunch before on the trek, but we merited it that day. We were all shaking off the shock and trying to make light of it. "I have never seen snow before," Fabiano exclaimed with an appropriately gleeful demeanor, albeit a delirious one. Gabriel lived in British Columbia, and he was very fit from rock climbing there. "That's quite an introduction to snow," he piped in. Gabriel made coffee for all of us, and then porters showed up from Perros, saying that they had turned 20 people back, and that ten more had turned around.

I said, "You mean the rangers sent them back?" "No," the porter said, "the porters have the authority." He told Fabiano that one girl started out in leggings and was sent back. Gabriel and Fabiano and I worried about the older couple David and Eileen, and hoped that they had turned back. They were wearing mesh hiking boots, not snow boots.

I was very worried about the remainder of the hike that day. It was still snowing, so I put my shell on over my down coat. On this day, I was as slow as I could have expected to be on a terrible Lyme day. My joints were swollen and they ached. My stomach throbbed from anxiety, and probably from the poorly digested Cuban black beans and rice I had stuffed into my mouth for extra calories the night before. My legs and feet were still soaking wet. My dry pants were soaked through, and I couldn't control my feet or ankles. That was a very odd sensation. They wouldn't move where I wanted them to move. My ankles half-twisted, and the terrain was very dangerous. The danger augmented because of the snow and the mystery of what lay beneath it. I was behind Fabiano and Gabriel, and I couldn't keep up. It was humiliating to make them wait; I begged them to go on without me.

It was like my body had been replaced with a decrepit one. I think I had tensed it up during my passage of survival, and then it became limp. I finally had to tell them to go on, and I told them so sternly that they left me. My pride was firmly intact, which Fabiano scolded me for later.

Our plan that night was to abandon our tents and reserve bunk beds with full board at the *refugio*, and drink wine together to celebrate being alive. I had seen my boat, the *Glacier Grey II*, approach the glacier far below us, like a little red speck, and Fabiano had said: "Look! It's your boat for tomorrow!" I told him that I would try to get on the 4:00 boat for today. When they went ahead, I cried a little. I did want them to go, and I was embarrassed at how slow I had become. I was also afraid to hike alone because I was in such bad shape with my lame feet and exhaustion.

Every single step was painful and hard. It reminded me of the physical journey Brady had been on in his fight to stay alive. I climbed cold metal ladders, crossed terrifying ravines over dangling suspension bridges, trudged through mud, slid down steep rocks, climbed steep rocks, and inched along over narrow ridges parallel to the immense glacier to my right. The steely sky did not welcome me to this side of the Andes. I could not take one photo because my hands were frozen and clumsy that day, and because it was raining so hard. I was worried that my iPhone would be ruined by the rain, and all my photos and the texts about Brady would be lost, but the Arcteryx protected it.

At long last, after one last frightening climb down a wet, steep ladder, I came to a sign that read "Refugio Grey." I sighed many sighs of relief, panted a little, and looked like a ghastly specter, I am sure. I went to check-in, but they said that there was no bed available. It was possible to rent a dry tent, but I only had soaking wet clothes and a wet sleeping bag, and there was no hot water until 7:00 p.m. Fabiano walked in the check-in building and hugged me. He was visibly delighted, and said proudly, "Gabriel said it would take you an hour or more, but it only took you 30 minutes more, I knew it!" I asked the check-in lady if I could take my vessel one day early at 4:00, because it was now 3:45, but she said to go to the next building at the Refugio desk.

I explained that I had already hiked 22 kilometers that day, that I was miserable, that the pass had nearly killed me, and I begged them to call the Hotel Grey to see if I could get on the boat. They were very sympathetic, and there was a lady who spoke English very well. "They should never have let you pass," she said. Her colleague radioed the vessel, it was now 3:55, and the boat was scheduled to depart at 4:00. The nice lady gave me a hot coffee, which I drank in gulps. Then she said not to wait for a radio response, but to race to the *Mirador Grey*, a 10-minute hike, to try to catch it while she radioed that I was on the way.

I raced (hobbled) to the check-in desk, calling out "Fabiano!" as I ran so that I would not miss saying farewell. I frantically found him at the check-in desk, and I hugged him, thanked him, and made a prayer sign with my hands while saying, "I will never forget." Then I half slung my backpack over my back, and race-hobbled in a frenzy. I didn't even stop to fasten my backpack around my waist or chest. I wasn't sure which way to go because the path forked. I went left, rushing down the path, not seeing a boat. When I saw the mast, I broke into a stumbling run until I could see sailors reaching down to take up the gangplank. I waved my arms, called out, and they gesticulated for me to come.

I ran across the black glacial sand on the beach, half-falling as I went. I blurted out feeble exclamations of gratitude when I got there. They helped me climb on the boat, took off my pack, stored it, and when the captain heard my story about the John Gardner Pass, he personally offered me a pisco sour. I didn't know what it was, but the bartender made it and it tasted like a delicious margarita. It was surreal to be there. The boat had funky house music playing softly, and it was full of civilized-looking people wearing lifejackets and sitting at booth tables on the boat. I couldn't acclimate to seeing 'real' people who hadn't been in the mountains. I had gone from hell to a party boat.

I took my pisco sour, made my way to a booth with an empty seat, and asked a friendly looking Australian family if I could join them. We shared our lives with one another, and I talked about the merits of reading with their 13-year-old daughter. After talking for a while, we went out with our lifejackets to photograph the glaciers up close. I have never been so grateful for anything. I really think it was a matter of life or death. I could not have lasted the night with no dry clothes. I was miserable and in pain, I couldn't wait to get off that mountain.

The nice Australians, Wendy, Neale, and Riley, walked me to their car, 30 minutes away from the boat. I would still have had to walk a lengthy distance to the hotel, but my new friends offered to drive me. Riley carried my pack to the car, and then they drove me to the Hotel Grey. They waited with me to make sure I had a room. What good Samaritans. Brady was looking out for me once again. It was 6:50 p.m. by the time that I got to my room.

I have never been so happy to be in a hotel room. It had a gigantic Scandinavian king-size bed with giant down pillows and a duvet. With swollen, still numb hands,

I fished out my toiletry bag. The shower was very hot, to my delight. I stripped off all of my wet clothes. Even my bra was soaking wet. I sat down on the expansive tiled shower floor, unable to stand, and I scrubbed my ailing body. I was seeing it for the first time since I had left the Hotel Torres. I had black and blues everywhere; I counted 32. My body seemed sinewy to me, as if I had become a hairless wild animal as I crossed the pass.

I could not get enough of the hot shower, and I washed each body part several times. I aimed the hose everywhere, especially on my cold back and feet. I brushed my teeth for a long time as the water poured over me. How decadent it seemed. Finally, I painfully stood up, with little balance. I dried my body and shuffled to the bed where I lay down under the duvet. I was so grateful to be safe, but my body was wracked with the trauma of the pass. I still felt like I was on the pass, like I was being blown by an invisible wind.

I wanted to skip dinner and pass out, but I knew I needed calories after the 24-kilometer hike I had done that day. I took my dried black base layer and base layer top from the radiator, covered them with my Patagonia blue vest, and put on my wet Birkenstocks with no socks, because I did not have one pair of dry socks. I laid out my wet tent and sleeping bag to dry.

Through the window at my table for one, I could see the lake, the glacier, the white mountains, and the hidden niche where the *refugio* would be. I raised my glass of Chilean Cabernet to Fabiano and Gabriel and took a picture. I felt sad that we couldn't celebrate. We had hiked together intermittently throughout the Torres del Paine, and Fabiano had helped me so much.

When I got back to my room, I direct dialed D. No answer. Then I direct dialed Dad. Janet sounded a million miles away, and I barely recognized her voice. "Janet! Janet!" When she knew it was me, she yelped and ran to get Dad. I told him, "I'm alive. I made it. I finished. I hiked 140 kilometers. I'm safe." He was so grateful I called, and he sounded like he was hyperventilating a little. I said goodbye and dozed off.

I woke up at 5:00 in disbelief that I didn't need to break down camp or start boiling water for that horrid oatmeal. I had dreamed that night that Brady was alive. Brady and I went for a long walk, and he had a lot of energy, and we walked in stride together as we always have. Then there was a party for him. Jim and Arthur were there with D, Dad, and Janet. I was going to call Dr. Kaddetz and say that there had been a big mistake. Brady didn't need to be put to sleep. It was a marvel. Then I woke up and remembered that I had been holding Brady when he died, so he must really be dead. Was he with me in that dream in spirit? Was I in denial? It was almost the same dream I had about Grandma. He was there in spirit, as was she. They both sandwiched me during my time of crisis. Without Fabiano and Gabriel, I would have surely died on the John Gardner Pass. I truly believe this. Others have died there before me.

I was disoriented, but I gently let my body sleep until I woke up, startled to see the digital numbers 8:11 on the electric alarm clock. *I'm back in civilization with electricity,* I remembered. When I rose, I realized that my feet and legs still didn't work well. My ankles and feet hurt terribly, and I never would have been able to hike today to finish the O. My O had a tiny piece missing because I took the boat at Refugio Grey and didn't hike back down to Paine del Grande, where I had started. Once again, perfectionist Miche would have been tormented by this incomplete O, but I accepted my hike as a major feat and I did not feel remorse.

I descended slowly to a breakfast of scrambled eggs and freshly brewed coffee that didn't come from a powder. I have been writing ever since, waiting for my van to the Hotel Singular to come.

I wrote discursively:

I think Fabiano saved my life. I have to thank him.

This park is for the pumas. The mountains are killer.

I thought the pass debilitated me. But no, it showed me I'm tough as nails.

I have incredible spirit protection. Thank you, Brady and Grandma.

I have honored my soulmate dog. I have started to grieve for him. That was my mission here.

Saturday, November 5

I found Fabiano last night at Erratic Rock basecamp in Puerto Natales. He was just sitting there facing the door when I walked in, framing the entire place. I'm so happy I got to say goodbye to him, and thank him for hiking with me. His face lit up with the joy of a pure child, although he is in a six-foot six-inch body. He was finishing a pizza and about to open a bottle of wine. We were able to talk through that horrible day. "Michelle, I cried when you got hypothermia. I thought you were going to die. It was awful. Your face was blue and pale, and you barely recognized us. You are a very strong girl." I thanked him over and over, and told him that one day I would come to Rio and take him and his wife out to dinner to celebrate that we lived through the John Gardner Paso. After he finished his wine, we hugged, and he departed from Patagonia right then and there.

November 5

I seem to be okay as long as I keep moving. I need to keep moving the stress, shock, loss, anxiety, and sadness out of my body. I feel disoriented since I got off the mountain, as if to ask, "What am I doing here in civilization among people — strangers — who do not know my loss and my experience."

Then D joined me. I had asked him to meet me in El Calafate on November 6th, and he was there.

November 9

D was walking with another American hiker he had met the day we hiked near Fitz Roy, and I descended alone. The trail was relatively flat, and the scenery of alpine bushes juxtaposed with snow-peaked mountains and copper and periwinkle plateaus appealed to all of my aesthetic senses.

I was quietly marveling at it when Brady came to me. He said these words very clearly: "Of course I was going to give you a big gift, a reward for being my nurse and healer." I shouldn't have been, but I was blown away. May I underscore that I do not have voices in my head; this was Brady's voice coming through loud and clear. I did deserve a big gift for being Brady's healer and nurse, didn't I? This could not have been a more perfect gift to thank me for the three years that I had nursed Brady through leptospirosis and chronic renal failure. Those three extra years were an extraordinary gift, too. "You are a fearless warrior for my health, and for that I am grateful," he had written in his letter. And this is how he showed his gratitude.

Just moments before, I had found a lone syringe in my down jacket pocket. This was not a down jacket that I had brought on my solo hike, rather it was a lightweight jacket D had brought to me from home as a change of gear, so I had not found it earlier. The needle was from one of Brady's saline fluids bags. For two weeks, and 160 kilometers I have not left one trace, but in this moment, I impulsively thrust the tightly capped needle into a low-lying bush. "No more needles for us, we don't need them now," I said out loud.

November 15

In Ushuaia, D and I packed a daypack, and took an early morning taxi to the trailhead of Laguna Esmeralda in the Tierra del Fuego region. The trail disappeared into the thick woods, and it was shaded and snow covered. Soon my thoughts turned to Brady. I thought that I couldn't feel Brady. I felt very alarmed that I had lost the connection.

A stunning black and white border collie appeared by my side; she had shining blue eyes brimming with friendly energy. She licked my hands and wagged her tail.

D was delighted to see her. "Hello, dog! Hello, dog!" he kept exclaiming. This dog was well maintained and well fed by the looks of her healthy coat, so I don't think that she was a stray dog. She started hiking with us. She gracefully extended her legs like a canine ballerina to leap over fallen trees off the trail in the woods. Then she'd turn back and check on us as we hiked the trail. Brady always used to do this. Her energy reminded me so much of youthful Brady and of all the hikes the three of us took together when he was a pup.

I thought Brady had sent her to us so that we could feel him. He sent her to remind me that he was hiking with us every step of the way.

Dog, we called her "Dog," stayed with us as we flew down the extremely muddy trail with her. We passed several hikers as the morning wore on, but she never left us to join another group. In fact, she hiked with me to the summit. It was superb. The sun was shining. I felt free from Lyme that day, and Brady was free from his body, and this beautiful free dog hiked with me.

D was several minutes behind, almost the whole way, but Dog stayed by my side. The trail was the muddiest I have ever been on. Sometimes my boot would become entirely submerged in the mud. The path was diverse. It meandered through passes with snowy winds, over peat bogs, up a mountainous steep path, along a watery, sun-drenched river, still ascending.

Finally, after two false camels — or deceptive summit sightings — we reached the view of the emerald laguna with a backdrop of perfectly framed white, rocky, mountains. It was as if we had stepped into Shangri-La. Dog bounded down to the laguna for a drink, before running back up to sit next to me. She seemed full of joy, and her eyes just shone at me. D joined us, panting and grunting after his belabored hike, and she greeted him with joy, too.

I looked down at my trousers and boots covered in mud and thought the obvious: sometimes you have to hike through mud to get to the beauty. I laughed. Laughter was a gift those days.

The mystery dog appears by our sides and hikes to Laguana Esmeralda with is in Patagonia.

All the way down, I kept passing other hikers that Dog could have joined, but she stayed with me. We walked Dog over to a sled dog facility near the trailhead, but the owners told us that she belonged to another family, she just frequently spent the day there with the sled dogs. We could return to Ushuaia with the knowledge that Dog was safe and sound.

When D and I were back in Ushuaia, gazing out over the strait that led to Antarctica, he handed me a card. It had a picture of a golden retriever on the outside, with a printed message reading, "As they say in obedience

213

school…" When I opened it, it said, "HEAL!" D had written the following:

Dear Michelle,

I am very glad you survived the long hike. Brady would be very impressed and proud of you. I had a long conversation with his spirit a few days ago… He really wants you to rally and focus on your other goals in life. I understand this period of your life isn't easy, but let's try to do all we can to slowly transition to another page. I am very excited about this long trip to Argentina, it should be full of discoveries for me.

XO & Love,

D.S.

I thanked D with my teary eyes. Brady would agree with it. It would take me a few months to "rally and focus on my other goals in life," as I had made caring for Brady my sole mission for quite some time. D would be the one to encourage me to write again. The healing journey would be like the hike in Patagonia.

December 15

Brady and I lived deeply, and we sucked the marrow out of life for nine years. Yet, like all those who grieve, I posed the dreaded "what if" question that had been plaguing me. "Did my quest for a miracle kill Brady? If I had not done the stem cell therapy, I wonder if he may have lived another year or two. Yet Brady was also tired, and we had been fighting for years. The venerable doctor did his very best.

I took a pause from these tortured contemplations to call Tiffany's and order a rose-gold heart locket engraved with a "B" to wear forever. I planned to put a lock of Brady's cream-colored cheek fur in it. The Tiffany's saleswoman Rita was kind when I told her an abridged story about Brady, and she said the locket was for closure. It really isn't for closure; it's a symbol I can wear to honor him and honor our bond. But there can be no closure on a love like that. No end. He is with me.

I am also with him. I can also send him light from wherever I am. I can also be there for him. Why didn't I think of that? When I made the realization that I am also with him, I played my special aria on alto saxophone for him, and I felt my heart full of his essence, palpably so.

On Brady's birthday, over oysters and champagne, D gave a makeshift toast to Brady: "To our very special boy. He brought a lot of love into our lives. You did a very good job with Brady," he said hesitantly. I was not able to sustain the conversation for long without weeping again, and D could hardly bear my ongoing tears. Bereavement is messy.

It was time for the next leg of D's operation Distract Michelle. He put me on a plane to Copenhagen to visit my close friend Liv who I had met at Dartmouth College. When Liv rolled up on her bike to meet me for coffee at one of our favorite coffee shops, she enveloped me, showing her sympathy through her intense chocolate eyes. Liv is very powerful in her convictions, which she shares at will. "Miche, life is short. You love dogs. You have to get another dog." I bowed my head and sighed. "Ah, but I am not ready, Liv. I can't just replace my soulmate dog."

"Miche, don't wait too long. You are best with a dog," she insisted.

My therapist said something very similar to me on the phone one day, "Miche, you should always have a dog. Brady keeps you grounded; he is like your therapy dog." Brady lapped up my pain and brought out the best in me.

When I tried to return home, I couldn't take being in Connecticut, so I drove to Brady's Retreat in the Berkshires to finish writing his book. During the drive, I remembered one of my last conversations with Debbie and Brady, in which Brady said, "The book isn't really finished because she hasn't figured out what picture of me to use. She should choose a photo of my eyes. My eyes are very special. My eyes are my message." I mentally scrolled through the thousands of photographs that I had organized as a Brady album in my iPhone. The one that arrested my attention was of Brady sitting placidly up in the Menil tree in Houston, with me smiling at his side as Arthur snapped the photograph. That photograph said it all, and as I crossed into snowy Massachusetts in mid-December, I vowed to place the Menil photo on the cover of Brady's book.

I was not ready for the raw grief that greeted me at Brady's Retreat; the silence of his absence sent me into another jeremiad. Everything had been more alive thanks to him. I woke up disoriented that Brady was not there by my bedside. There was no reason to go outside to throw his ball down the hillside and traipse around the yard in the fresh snow. I stood outside with my coffee, out of habit — confused — as if I were waiting for Brady to do his business.

When I went to my desk to write, I started sobbing and howling. I lay my pen down, dropped my head, and pressed my cheek into my notebook. How would I go on without Brady? I wrote about it: "I am hollow. I ache for BD. My sorrow is so deep that I cannot bear it. I wail so hard that my heart shakes. I just want to caress his fur, gaze at him, walk through the snow and exist together. How will this ever get better?"

I paused to breathe, like Vijaya had taught me. I remembered the wise words of David Kessler and Elizabeth Kübler-Ross that went something like this: depression is an appropriate response to a great loss.[64] Vijaya had advised me: "When the sadness and depression come in, breathe in his love. Install him in your heart." I clutched the rose-gold heart-shaped locket on my chest and closed my eyes. Suddenly those words from the Snatam Kaur song I sang to Brady in the hospital were meant for me: "May the pure light within you guide you." My peace was authentic for the first time, although I would continue to grieve. I learned that interspecies love does not expire with spent bodies. May these words also console you, dear readers who may be grieving for your canine soul mates. Soul mate love is a forever love.

Epilogue

In Memory of Brady

Michelle Slater: "Brady will always be my soulmate dog. I loved him as much as anyone ever loved anyone. I could never get enough of him."

Dr. Mike Bartholomew: "Brady is a miracle dog. He is one of the highlights of my career as a veterinarian."

Jim Lowe, friend in Vermont: "A dog was never better loved. Hell, a person was never better loved."

Dr. Nate Heilman: "What an incredible creature and a teacher for me. I'll never, ever forget him."

Aunt Beast: "Brady was loving, protective, and independent-minded."

Debbie McGillivray: "Brady is absolutely brilliant. He is a brilliant being."

Courtney, technician, Pound Ridge Vet: "Brady was a very special soul. He touched my heart in a special way."

Hannah Kezema, Brady's caretaker: "Brady will forever leave a special paw print on my heart."

Jonni Lynch, childhood friend from Interlochen; lover of dogs: "This little love… that turned into one so large to block the sun. Brady was brave and beloved."

Vijaya Nair: "Brady gave you the greatest gift! He is an extraordinary being. His love for you is so big."

Meredith Kilgore, participant in the animal

communication workshop: "Soul mates. Miche and Brady are soul mates."

Louise Jones, friend of Brady: "A beautiful friend we won't forget."

Nancy Capel, neighbor in Conn. and friend of Brady: "You took such good care of your boy and Brady loved you so much."

Rainy Broomfield, neighbor in Conn. and friend of Brady: "He was the most magnificent dog and more human than canine." "He was one of the most magnificent creatures I have ever met and he was so cherished."

Aimee Quaife, neighbor in Wis. and friend of Brady: "We'll always treasure those special memories of happy, sweet Brady"

Tyler Clark, childhood friend from Interlochen: "He was one of the most beautiful creatures I ever met, and I'm so grateful I had that opportunity."

Kathy Delano, interior designer, Conn. "It's hard to believe such a strong, majestic creature is gone so soon."

Cate Marvin, Mayapple Center professor and friend of Brady: "Brady was such a wonder."

Chris Onthank: "Michelle was Brady's soul mate."

Isabel Sutter, Brady's caretaker in Houston and friend of Brady: "I kept photos of Brady on my phone. Whenever I felt unhappy I would play this live photo of him licking me in your backyard. He had so much love to give, and he bestowed it so generously. You took the best care of him—y'all were meant to be together and he loved you so much."

Rell Iacono, Mayapple Center poet: "Brady truly was a light."

Jonathan Rezach, former student at Univ. of WI and caretaker of Brady: "Brady was an amazing dog and spirit."

Arthur Zorn: "Brady was a true spiritual essence. He guarded and guided us to the light and unknown dimensions of time of space. Brady, we thank you."

Jeannette Patterson, colleague at Johns Hopkins and lover of animals: "Miche and Brady had something really special."

D: "Brady was a character. He was very playful. He was very protective of Michelle. He picked up on her energy. He was very affectionate. Although he listened to Michelle, he was very independent-minded. He was good-looking like me, but he took his eating habits after Michelle, meaning he was a very picky eater."

Dr. Kaddatz: "You did so right by Brady and he knew it."

Chris, Pound Ridge vet: "What a gentle soul he was."

Dr. Mike: "The beauty of Brady's case is that he had a team that was willing to go the distance with him. This included his veterinary team, you, and most importantly Brady. There were many times along this journey when both you and he could have given up. I truly believe that his will stayed strong because he had such positive support. I see many cases in which the positive (or negative) attitude from the owner affects the patient demeanor and outcome of the case."

Michael Slater: "Brady was the most intelligent and beautiful dog I have ever known."

Sudeep Moniz, colleague of D, caretaker of Brady: "Brady was a wonderful companion full of personality, he had the best life cared for by Michelle and D. They were both incredible parents."

SOULMATE DOG

Janet Slater: "Free dog... may our precious Jolly Ball dog rest in peace. Much loved Brady will live on in our hearts and memories forever and be enormously missed. Blessed are we to have had him in our lives."

ACKNOWLEDGMENTS

The gratitude I have for those who played critical roles in Brady's life will always live in me. However, I would like to credit them again here, and thank those who have brought *Soulmate Dog* into the world from behind the scenes.

Without Dmitri Sinenko, I couldn't have cared for Brady as I did, and I'm grateful that D loved and supported Brady just as much as I did. Team Brady was nothing short of exceptional, so I thank once again Kathleen Abbott, Arthur Zorn, and Brady's tireless grandparents Janet Slater, and the late Michael Slater. For the specialists at VCA, most notably Dr. Beth Whitney, who saw Brady through his acute stage of renal failure, I am still grateful and relieved. I will never forget Brady's personal St. Francis, Dr. Nate Heilman, for whom we have tremendous respect. Dr. Whitney and Dr. Heilman saved Brady's life and I am indebted to them. Thank you to Debbie McGillivray who enlightened me about who Brady really was and what he could say; Debbie changed my perspective on animals forever. I will always be grateful to Debbie for supporting Brady through his crisis at the emergency hospital and beyond. Thank you to Chris Onthank for helping me to train Brady when he was traumatized (and independent-minded), and for bringing his vivacious spirit back. There are countless others who I have to thank when it comes to Brady.

On the writing and book production side, I would like to thank my brilliant editor, Carrie Frye, who helped me see the importance of writing about my early grief before I told Brady's story; Carrie helped me shape *Soulmate Dog* into what it is today. Without my audio book publisher

Alison Larkin and her extraordinary belief in *Soulmate Dog*, I'm not sure how it would have reached my readers. Alison's tireless promoting of *Soulmate Dog* has brought it from my hard drive to the world. I would like to thank publisher Colin Mustful for his willingness to take on *Soulmate Dog* in a new imprint. I'm thankful to my talented publicists David Hahn and Adrienne Fontaine for bringing *Soulmate Dog* to larger audiences. Thank you to my friend Susan Doheny who procured permissions for *Soulmate Dog*. Lastly, I honor the great love for animals I shared with my beloved late parents, Michael and Euphemia Slater. Michael Slater was the best grandparent to Brady that he could have wished for.

APPENDIX

As an integrative practitioner, I've learned not to judge a patient based simply on a piece of paper. It all goes into the database, but if the patient has the will to carry on and is maintaining a good quality of life, we continue to support them in their journey.
                                                    –Dr. Mike Bartholomew

Extraordinary Resources for Canines

Extraordinary Veterinarians:

Dr. Nathan Heilman, Qi Vet
http://qiveterinaryclinic.com

Smith Ridge Vet
http://smithridge.com

Dr. Mike Bartholomew, Animal Hospital of Dunedin Veterinarians
http://www.ahofd.com/dunedin-veterinarians/

Kidney Specialists: Animal Medical Center
http://www.amcny.org

UC California Davis Vet Center
http://www.vetmed.ucdavis.edu/index.cfm

Animal Communication:

Debbie McGillivray - Animal Communicator & Author
www.animaltelepathy.com

Supplements:

https://iheartdogs.com/

http://shop.mercola.com/category/384/1/pets

Homeopathy:

https://www.homeopathyforanimals.com/

Therapies for Animals:

International Association of Animal Massage & Bodywork/ Association of Canine Water Therapy - Directory of Individual Professional Members providing services in water therapy, massage therapy, and bodywork
https://iaamb.org/directory/iaambacwt-individual-professional-members/#!directory/map/ord=lnm

National Board of Certification for Animal Acupressure and Massage - Certified Practitioner List for Acupressure and Massage in the USA, Canada, and New Zealand
http://www.nbcaam.org/

Aqua Therapy :

Jody Chiquoine - Certified Canine Rehabilitation Therapist
http://fittercritters.org/

Also: See Book Resources for Jody Chiquoine

Integrative Veterinary Center - CA
http://integrativeveterinarycenter.com/services/cancer-therapies/
An excellent site enumerating and explaining alternative healing therapies:
   Vitamin C drip therapy
   Laser therapy
   Chinese Herbal Medicine
   Animal Chiropractic
   Acupuncture

Please ask your veterinarian about Massage, Qi Gong, and Reiki as well.

Health Insurance Companies:

Many options are available for pet insurance. The North

American Pet health Insurance Association (NAPHIA) is comprised of reputable pet health insurance (PHI) organizations from across Canada and the United States. NAPHIA's membership makes up over 99% of all pet health insurance coverage in effect in North America. https://naphia.org/

Crowd Funding:

www.plumfund.com - Plumfund's fundraising website is designated to help anyone raise money online for an animal or pet in need. Raise funds for veterinary care, medication, x-rays, physical therapy, and emergency hospital stays

Rescues:

Please consider rescuing a dog through your local ASPCA chapter or Humane Society

Book Resources:

A Dog Lover's Guide to Canine Massage, by Jody Chiquoine and Linda Jackson

The Complete Idiot's Guide to Pet Psychic Communication by Debbie McGillivray

Untamed Voices: If you Speak They will Listen by Debbie McGillivray and Sue Steffens

Animal Communication Boot Camp by Debbie McGillivray

The Nature of Animal Healing by Dr. Martin Goldstein, D.V.M

NOTES

1   Robert Franklin Leslie, *In the Shadow of a Rainbow,* (New York: W.W.Norton, 1974), 159

2   Martin Amis, *Inside Story: A Novel,* (New York: Alfred A. Knopf, 2020), xv

3   Boris Cyrulnik, *Resilience,* (New York: Penguin Books, 2009), 1

4   From *The Unbearable Lightness of Being* by Milan Kundera. English translation copyright © 1984 by Harper & Row, Publishers, Inc. Translated from Nesnesitelná lehkost by tí, copyright © 1984 by Milan Kundera. Used by permission of HarperCollins Publishers.

5   Ibid., 289.

6   Donna Haraway, *When Species Meet,* (Minneapolis: University of Minnesota Press,2008), 49

7   Ibid,. 60.

8   Martin Buber, *I and Thou,* trans. Ronald Gregor Smith, (New York: Charles Scriber's Sons, 1958), 96-97

9   McDermott, R. "Profile Ray L. Birdwhistell," The Kinesis Report, 1980, 2, 3:1-16

10 Gregory Bateson, *Steps to An Ecology of Mind,* (Chicago: The University of Chicago Press, 1972), 13

11 Ibid., 190.

12 Jaak Panksepp, *Affective Neuroscience: The Foundations of Human and Animal Emotions.* (New York: Oxford University Press, 1998)

13 Mark Derr, *How the Dog Became the Dog: From Wolves to our Best Friends,* (Overlook Press: New York, 2011), 129

14 William James, "What Psychical Research Has Accomplished," Forum: August, 1892, 727-742, 737-738.

15 Ibid.

16 Michel de Montaigne, (*Apologie de Raymond Sebond,* Paris:

Gallimard, 1950), 498-505 (translation mine)

17 J. Allen Boone, *Kinship with All Life,* (New York: Harper & Row, 1954), 72

18 Raymond Coppinger, Mark Feinstein, *How Dogs Work,* (Chicago: The University of Chicago Press, 2015), 199

19 Sy Montgomery, "Psychological Effects of Pets are Profound," The Boston Globe, January 12, 2015

20 Ibid.

21 Americans spend more than fifteen billion dollars per year on family animal care. Although sixty-eight percent of households have family members that are animals, to my astonishment, only one percent of these animals are insured. As a New York Times article from January 9, 2017 underscores, however, "the point of health insurance is to protect against the risk of catastrophically high costs." In spite of this recent growth, Consumer Reports concluded in 2016 that pet insurance is not a good value unless one's animal companion has expensive medical costs.

22 Sean D. Kelly, "Waking Up To The Gift of Aliveness," The New York Times, December 25, 2017

23 Jacques Derrida, *The Animal That Therefore I am,* trans. David Wills, (Fordham: Fordham University Press,2008), 56

24 Ludwig Wittgenstein, *Philosophical Investigations,* Trans. G.E.M. Anscombe, (Oxford: Blackwell Publishing, 2001), 77e

25 Haraway, *When Species Meet,*79

26 Matthew Calarco, *Zoographies: The Question of the Animal from Heidegger to Derrida,* (New York: Columbia University Press, 2008), 1, Reprinted with permission of Columbia University Press.

27 Haraway, *When Species Meet,* 152

28 Jan Narveson, "Animal Rights," *The Canadian Journal of Philosophy 7,* no. 1:161-178, Jan. 1977

29 Jeske, Diane, "Special Obligations", *The Stanford Encyclopedia of Philosophy* (Spring 2014 Edition), Edward N. Zalta (ed.), URL   =   <https://plato.stanford.edu/archives/spr2014/entries/special-obligations/>.

30 J.M. Coetzee, *The Lives of Animals,* (Princeton: Princeton University Press, 1999), 23

31 Jeremy Bentham, *Introduction to the Principles of Morals and Legislation,* (Oxford: Clarendon Press, 1789), 310

32 Ibid., 311.

33 In a 2011 draft of the Universal Declaration of Animal Rights, set forth by UNESCO in Paris on the 15th of October, 1978, article five states that any animal who is dependent on a human has the right to proper sustenance and care, and shall not be neglected, abandoned, or killed. Although several proposals have been drafted and circulated as petitions, the United Nations has not endorsed the Declaration of Animal Rights.

34 In fact, in the furthest-advancing animal rights case in U.S. history, New York's highest court ruled on June 14, 2022 that a highly intelligent elephant at the Bronx Zoo, Happy, is not a person and is therefore not entitled to the rights of habeas corpus. As a nonhuman animal, Happy then remains classified as a thing.

35 Cary Wolfe, Natasha Lennard, "Is Humanism Really Humane?" *The New York Times,* Jan. 9, 2017

36 Cary Wolfe, *What is Posthumanism?,* (Minneapolis: University of Minnesota Press, 2010, xiv-xvii

37 Ibid.

38 Ibid.

39 I want to point out that although Brady would be considered a companion animal, I didn't distinguish Brady in comparison with other animals such as farmed animals or wild animals, but I don't want to broach this subject as it is problematic in the field of animal studies, and merits more attention than what I could give it here.

40 Ibid. 9

41 Derrida is so disgruntled with the baggage-laden term "animal" that he calls for replacing it with the word *animot* – a made-up word in French—a Derridean neologism that contests the limit between animals and humans. He uses the suffix *–mot,* or 'word' in French, to imply that animals are not deprived of language after all, which would, eventually, have radical implications when taking animal communication into consideration.

42 Jacques Derrida, "Violence Against Animals," in *For What*

Tomorrow...: A Dialogue, by Jacques Derrida and Elizabeth Roudinesco, trans. Jeff Fort (Stanford, CA: Stanford University Press, 2004), 63

43   Ibid. 27

44   Jacques Derrida, *Memoirs for Paul de Man.* Trans. C. Lindsay, J. Culler, E. Cadava, and P. Kamuf, (New York: Columbia University Press, 1989), 28, Reprinted with permission of Columbia University Press.

45   Milan Kundera, *The Unbearable Lightness of Being,* Trans. Michael Henry Heim, (New York: Harper Collins, 1999), 287

46   Jean-Luc Nancy, *The Inoperative Community,* (Minnesota: University of Minnesota Press, 1991,) 85

47   Stanley Cavell, *Philosophy the Day After Tomorrow,* (Cambridge, Mass.: The Belknap Press of Harvard University Press, 2005), 151, Used by permission. All rights reserved.

48   Hélène Cixous, *Stigmata: Escaping Texts,* (New York: Routledge, 1998,) 186

49   Ibid.

50   Sydney Landon Plum, *Solitary Goose,* (Athens: University of Georgia Press, 2007), 25

51   Stanley Cavell, *The Claim of Reason,* (New York: Oxford University Press, 1979), 178

52   Eduardo Cadava, Peter Connor, Jean-Luc Nancy, Editors, *Who Comes After the Subject?,* (New York: Routledge, 1991), 116

53   Cary Wolfe, "Human, All Too Human: 'Animal Stuides' and the Humanities," *PMLA:* 124:2, March 2009, 571

54   Raymond Coppinger, Mark Feinstein, *How Dogs Work,* (Chicago: The University of Chicago Press, 2015), 197

55   Mark Rowlands, *The Philosopher and the Wolf,* (New York: Pegasus Books, 2010), 187

56   Stacey O'Brien, *Wesley the Owl:* (Atria Books, 2009)

57   Barbara Smuts, in *The Lives of Animals,* J.M. Coetzee (Princeton: Princeton University Press, 1999)115-120

58   Murasaki Shikibu, *The Tale of Genji,* Trans. Edward G. Seidensticker, (New York: Alfred A. Knopf, 1992), 788

59   Elisabeth Kübler-Ross and David Kessler, *On Grief and Grieving,* (New York: Scribner, 2005), xi

60   Ibid., 39.

61   Stanley Cavell, *In Quest of the Ordinary: Lines of Skepticism and Romanticism,* (Chicago: University of Chicago Press, 1998), 8

62   Kessler, Kübler-Ross, *On Grief and Grieving,* 207

63   Martin   Heidegger,   the   twentieth-century   German philosopher and scion of thought on existence, argues that the animals don't have a full identity because they don't exist fully as humans do. In other words, he claims that domestic pets *live* with us but not in the sense that they are *being,* or *existing,* because "a dog does not exist but merely lives" [*ein Hund nicht existiert, sondern nur lebt.*] Since Heidegger did not have empirical evidence of animals' profound depth at hand, I do not fault him for limiting their faculties given his limited information, but I do not think he should ever be considered the authority on the philosophy of being. Since they aren't able to contemplate, be conscious or reason, they are merely alive without existing, therefore they don't leave behind an essence when they "croak." Without reason or consciousness, they do not even die, they merely croak. Brady certainly did not croak. He was acutely conscious that he was dying, and he reasoned as he reached over to lick my face and put his nose in my mouth. His essence is so strong, it still overcomes me.

64   Ibid., 20-24.

Printed in the USA
CPSIA information can be obtained
at www.ICGtesting.com
LVHW090430210624
783560LV00008B/871